T0273443

2ND EDITION

Trees *of the* Carolinas

Field Guide

Stan Tekiela

Adventure Publications
Cambridge, Minnesota

Dedication

In memory of my father.

Edited by Sandy Livoti and Ritchey Halphen

Cover, book design and leaf illustrations by Jonathan Norberg

Tree illustrations by Julie Martinez

Photo credits by photographer and page number:

Cover photo: White Oak by Stan Tekiela

All photo copyright by Stan Tekiela unless otherwise noted.

Steven J. Baskauf: 140 (main), 168 (fruit), 280 (fruit); **Rick and Nora Bowers:** 44 (bark), 46 (bark, main), 62 (immature fruit), 66 (flower), 120 (all), 192 (main), 196 (flower); **Dembinsky Photo Associates:** 296 (bark); **Dominique Braud/DPA*:** 82 (fruit); **Will Cook:** 44 (main), 58 (all), 76 (fruit), 116 (bark, immature fruit, main), 118 (bark, main), 144 (flower), 148 (flower, main), 154 (flower, fruit, main), 164 (fruit), 178 (flower, fruit, main), 186 (main), 188 (all), 194 (flower, fruit), 228 (all), 242 (bark, main), 250 (fruit), 252 (bark, main), 258 (fruit), 280 (main), 290 (bark, main), 312 (flower); **E. R. Degginger/DPA*:** 102 (fruit); **Dudley Edmondson:** 62 (all), 82 (flower), 112 (main), 168 (bark, main), 192 (bark), 196 (bark, fruit, main), 212 (fruit), 220 (bark, flower, main), 224 (bark, main), 246 (flower), 276 (flower); **Chris Evans:** 30 (bark), 122 (main), 142 (bark, main), 148 (bark), 176 (bark, flower, main); **Michael P. Gadomski/DPA*:** 284 (main); **H. Garrett/DPA*:** 212 (flower); **Carl Hunter@USDA-NRCS PLANTS Database:** 290 (fruit); **Jerry and Barb Jividen:** 284 (bark); **Bruce Kirchoff:** 116 (fruit); **Larry Kornhak:** 4 (cone, knees), 42 (all), 44 (cone), 46 (cone), 122 (bark, fruit), 148 (fruit), 154 (bark), 176 (fruit), 178 (bark), 186 (bark), 242 (fruit), 320 (bark, boots, fruit, main); **Robert Mirabello:** 30 (cone); and **David Wisse/DPA*:** 196 (fruit).

*Dembinsky Photo Associates

Photo credits continued on page 327

10 9 8 7 6 5 4

Trees of the Carolinas Field Guide
First Edition 2007
Second Edition 2020
Copyright © 2007 and 2020 by Stan Tekiela
Published by Adventure Publications
An imprint of AdventureKEEN
330 Garfield Street South
Cambridge, Minnesota 55008
(800) 678-7006
www.adventurepublications.net
All rights reserved
Printed in China
ISBN 978-1-64755-071-4 (pbk.), 978-1-64755-072-4 (ebook)

TABLE OF CONTENTS

THE CAROLINAS AND TREES

The Carolinas are great places for anyone interested in trees. With *Trees of the Carolinas Field Guide*, you'll be able to quickly identify 160 of the most common trees in North and South Carolina–nearly all of which are native to the two states. This guide also includes a number of common non-native trees that have been naturalized in the Carolinas. This book makes no attempt to identify cultivated or nursery trees.

Because this book is a unique all photographic guide just for the Carolinas, you won't have to page through photographs of trees that don't grow in the two states, or attempt to identify live trees by studying black-and-white line drawings.

WHAT IS A TREE?

For the purposes of this book, a tree is defined as a large woody perennial plant, usually with a single erect trunk, standing at least 15 feet (4.5 m) tall, with a well-defined crown. *Trees of the Carolinas Field Guide* helps you observe some basic characteristics of trees so you can identify different species confidently.

HOW THIS BOOK IS ORGANIZED

To identify a tree, you'll want to start by looking at the thumb tabs in the upper right-hand corner of the text pages. These tabs define the sections of the book. They combine several identifying features of a tree (main category, needle or leaf type and attachment) into one icon.

It's possible to identify trees using this field guide without learning about categories, leaf types and attachments. Simply flip through the pages to match your sample to the features depicted on the thumb tabs. Once you find the correct section, use the photos to find your tree. Or you may want to learn more about the features of trees in a methodical way, using the following steps to narrow your choices to just a few photos.

1. First, determine the appropriate section and find the right icon by asking these questions: Is the tree coniferous or deciduous? If it is a conifer, are the needles single, clustered or scaly? If it is deciduous, is the leaf type simple, lobed or compound, and do leaves attach to twigs in an opposite or alternate pattern?

2. Next, simply browse through the photos in that section to find your tree. Or, to further narrow your choices, use the icon in the lower right-hand corner of the text pages. These icons are grouped by the general shape of the needle or leaf, and increase in size as the average size of the needle or leaf increases.

3. Finally, by examining the full-page photos of needles or leaves, studying the inset photos of bark, flowers, fruit or other special features and considering information on text pages, you should be able to confidently identify the tree.

While these steps briefly summarize how you can use this book, it is quite helpful to learn more about how the sections are grouped by reading the Identification Step-by-Step section.

IDENTIFICATION STEP-BY-STEP
Conifer or Deciduous

Trees in this field guide are first grouped into two main categories that consist of 28 conifers and 132 deciduous trees.

Trees with evergreen needles that remain on branches year-round and have seeds in cones are conifers. Some examples of these are pines and spruces. There are a few conifers, such as the Bald Cypress and the Tamarack, that behave like deciduous trees, shedding all of their needles each fall. Trees with broad flat leaves that fall off their branches each autumn are deciduous. Some examples of these are oaks and maples.

You will see by looking at the thumb tabs that trees with needles (conifers) are shown in the first sections of the book, followed by trees with leaves (deciduous).

Needle or Leaf Type

CONIFER GROUP:
Single, Clustered or Scaly Needles

SINGLE   **CLUSTERED**   **SCALY**
(Range of
2–30 needles)

If the tree is a conifer, the next step is to distinguish among single, clustered and scaly needles. Begin by checking the number of needles that arise from one point. If you see only one needle arising from one point, look in the single needle section. Coniferous trees with single needles are shown first. If there are at least two needles arising from one point, turn to the clustered needles section. This second section is organized by the number of needles in a cluster. If you are trying to identify needles that overlap each other and have a scale-like appearance unlike the other needles, you will find this type in the scaly needles section.

DECIDUOUS GROUP:
Simple, Lobed or Compound

SIMPLE   **LOBED**   **COMPOUND**   **TWICE COMPOUND**   **PALMATE COMPOUND**

If the tree is deciduous, the next step is to determine the leaf type. Many of the simple leaves have a basic shape such as oval, round, oblong or triangular. Other simple leaves are lobed, identified by noticeable indentations along their edges. Simple leaves without lobes are grouped first, followed by the lobed leaf groups.

If a leaf is composed of smaller leaflets growing along a single stalk, you'll find this type in the compound leaf sections. When a leaf has small leaflets growing along the edge of a thinner secondary stalk, which is in turn attached to a thicker main stalk, check the twice compound section. If the leaf has leaflets emerging from a common central point at the end of a leafstalk, look in the palmate compound section.

Leaf Attachment

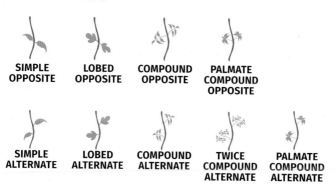

SIMPLE OPPOSITE   **LOBED OPPOSITE**   **COMPOUND OPPOSITE**   **PALMATE COMPOUND OPPOSITE**

SIMPLE ALTERNATE   **LOBED ALTERNATE**   **COMPOUND ALTERNATE**   **TWICE COMPOUND ALTERNATE**   **PALMATE COMPOUND ALTERNATE**

For deciduous trees, once you have determined the appropriate leaf type, give special attention to the pattern in which the leaves are attached to the twig. Trees with leaves that attach directly opposite of each other on a twig are grouped first in each section, followed by trees with leaves that attach alternately. The thumb tabs are labeled "opposite" or "alternate" to reflect the attachment group. All the above features (main category, needle or leaf type and attachment) are depicted in one icon for easy use.

Needle or Leaf Size

Once you have found the correct section by using the thumb tabs, note that the section is further loosely organized by needle or leaf size from small to large. Size is depicted in the needle or leaf icon located in the lower right-hand corner of text pages. This icon also reflects the shape of the needle or leaf. For example, the icon for the Amur Maple, which has a leaf size of 2–4 inches (5–10 cm), is smaller than the icon for the Norway Maple with a leaf size of 5–7 inches (12.5–18 cm). Measurement of any deciduous leaf extends from the base of the leaf (excluding the leafstalk) to the tip.

Using Photos and Icons to Confirm the Identity

After using the thumb tabs to narrow your choices, the last step is to confirm the tree's identity. First, compare the full-page photo of the leaves and twigs to be sure they look similar. Next, study the color and texture of the bark, and compare it to the inset photo. Then consider the information given about the habitat and range.

Sometimes, however, it is a special characteristic, such as flowers, fruit or thorns (described and/or pictured), that is an even better indicator of the identity. In general, if it's spring, check for flowers. During summer, look for fruit. In autumn, note the fall color.

Another icon is also included for each species to show the overall shape of the average mature tree, and how its height compares with a two-story house. For trees with an average height of more than 50 feet (15 m), this icon is shown on a slightly smaller scale.

STAN'S NOTES

Stan's Notes is fun and fact-filled with many gee-whiz tidbits of interesting information, such as historical uses, other common names and much more. Most information given in this descriptive section cannot be found in other tree field guides.

CAUTION

In Stan's Notes, it's occasionally mentioned that parts of some trees were used for medicine or food. While some find this interesting, DO NOT use this field guide to identify edible or medicinal trees. Certain trees in the Carolinas have toxic properties or poisonous look-alikes that can cause severe problems. Do not take the chance of making a mistake. Please enjoy the trees of the Carolinas with your eyes, nose or camera. In addition, please don't pull off leaves, cut branches or attempt to transplant any trees. Nearly all of the trees you will see are available at your local garden centers. These trees have been cultivated and have not been uprooted from the wild. Trees are an important part of our natural environment, and leaving a healthy tree unharmed will do a great deal to help keep North and South Carolina the wondrous places they are.

Enjoy the Trees!

LEAF BASICS

It's easier to identify trees and communicate about them when you know the names of the different parts of a leaf. For instance, it is more effective to use the word "sinus" to indicate an indentation on an edge of a leaf than to try to describe it.

The following illustrations show coniferous needles in cross section and the basic parts of deciduous leaves. The simple/lobed leaf and compound leaf illustrations are composites of leaves and should not be confused with any actual leaf of a real tree.

Needle Cross Sections

square   flat   triangular   round

Simple/Lobed Leaf

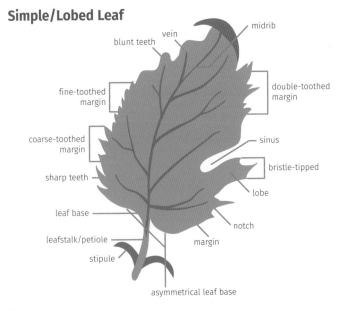

vein
midrib
blunt teeth
double-toothed margin
fine-toothed margin
coarse-toothed margin
sinus
bristle-tipped
sharp teeth
lobe
leaf base
notch
leafstalk/petiole
margin
stipule
asymmetrical leaf base

Compound Leaf

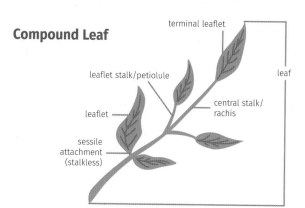

terminal leaflet

leaflet stalk/petiolule

leaf

central stalk/rachis

leaflet

sessile attachment (stalkless)

FINDING YOUR TREE IN A SECTION

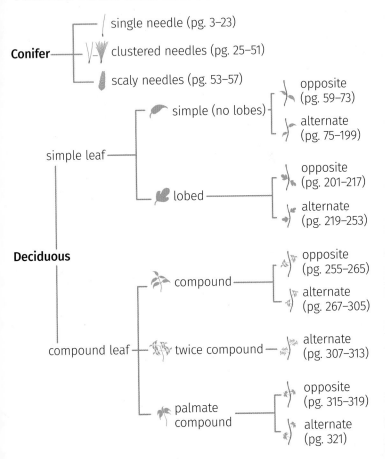

Conifer
- single needle (pg. 3–23)
- clustered needles (pg. 25–51)
- scaly needles (pg. 53–57)

Deciduous
- simple leaf
  - simple (no lobes)
    - opposite (pg. 59–73)
    - alternate (pg. 75–199)
  - lobed
    - opposite (pg. 201–217)
    - alternate (pg. 219–253)
- compound leaf
  - compound
    - opposite (pg. 255–265)
    - alternate (pg. 267–305)
  - twice compound
    - alternate (pg. 307–313)
  - palmate compound
    - opposite (pg. 315–319)
    - alternate (pg. 321)

The smaller needles and leaves tend to be toward the front of each section, while larger sizes can be found toward the back. Check the icon in the lower right corner of text pages to compare relative size.

SILHOUETTE QUICK COMPARES

To quickly narrow down which mature tree you've found, compare its rough outline with the samples found here. For a sense of scale, we've included the tree's height range compared with a drawing of a typical U.S. house. Obviously, tree heights and general shapes can vary significantly across individuals, but this should help you rule out some possible options, hopefully pointing you in the right direction. Once you've found a possible match, turn to the specified page and confirm or rule it out by examining the photos of bark and leaves and the accompanying text.

Common Prickly-ash
5–15'
pg. 279

Poison Sumac
5–20'
pg. 297

American Plum
10–15'
pg. 133

Sand Live Oak
10–15'
pg. 117

Wild Apple
10–15'
pg. 103

Buttonbush
10–20'
pg. 67

Chinese Privet
10–20'
pg. 59

Crab Apple
10–20'
pg. 101

European Buckthorn
10–20'
pg. 61

Juneberry
10–20'
pg. 159

Mountain-laurel
10–20'
pg. 165

Pussy Willow
10–20'
pg. 113

Russian-olive
10–20'
pg. 153

Smooth Sumac
10–20'
pg. 299

Staghorn Sumac
10–20'
pg. 301

Pin Cherry
10–30'
pg. 135

Striped Maple
10–30'
pg. 215

Amur Maple
15–20'
pg. 201

SILHOUETTE QUICK COMPARES, *continued*

Blue Beech
15–25'
pg. 167

Eastern Redbud
15–25'
pg. 175

European Mountain-ash
15–25'
pg. 275

Hawthorn
15–25'
pg. 157

American Mountain-ash
15–30'
pg. 277

Wax-myrtle
15–30'
pg. 155

American Bladdernut
20–25'
pg. 257

Common Hoptree
20–25'
pg. 267

Eastern Wahoo
20–25'
pg. 65

Devil's-walkingstick
20–30'
pg. 313

Eastern Flowering Dogwood
20–30'
pg. 63

Mountain Maple
20–30'
pg. 203

Pawpaw
20–30'
pg. 197

Red Mulberry
20–30'
pg. 173

Witch-hazel
20–30'
pg. 185

Carolina Ash
20–40'
pg. 259

Carolina Silverbell
20–40'
pg. 177

Fringetree
20–40'
pg. 69

Ironwood
20–40'
pg. 163

Ohio Buckeye
20–40'
pg. 319

Sweetbay
20–40'
pg. 145

Table Mountain Pine
20–40'
pg. 25

Turkey Oak
20–40'
pg. 243

Yellowwood
20–40'
pg. 269

Alternate-leaf Dogwood
25–35'
pg. 171

Blackjack Oak
25–40'
pg. 227

Black Spruce
25–50'
pg. 13

Eastern Redcedar
25–50'
pg. 53

Common Persimmon
30–40'
pg. 181

Fraser Fir
30–40'
pg. 21

Osage-orange
30–40'
pg. 183

Black Locust
30–50'
pg. 271

Boxelder
30–50'
pg. 255

Cabbage Palmetto
30–50'
pg. 321

Eastern Whitecedar
30–50'
pg. 55

Live Oak
30–50'
pg. 121

Sand Hickory
30–50'
pg. 281

Siberian Elm
30–50'
pg. 75

Sourwood
30–50'
pg. 195

Southern Catalpa
30–50'
pg. 71

Water Locust
30–50'
pg. 307

Winged Elm
30–50'
pg. 77

Post Oak
30–60'
pg. 233

Sassafras
30–60'
pg. 221

Virginia Pine
30–60'
pg. 27

Scotch Pine
30–80'
pg. 29

American Holly
40–60'
pg. 161

Austrian Pine
40–60'
pg. 33

SILHOUETTE QUICK COMPARES, *continued*

Black Oak
40–60'
pg. 245

Black Willow
40–60'
pg. 115

Butternut
40–60'
pg. 305

Carolina Basswood
40–60'
pg. 189

Carolina Hemlock
40–60'
pg. 7

Colorado Spruce
40–60'
pg. 17

Cucumbertree
40–60'
pg. 147

Eastern Hemlock
40 60'
pg. 9

Gingko
40–60'
pg. 151

Hackberry
40–60'
pg. 105

Honey Locust
40–60'
pg. 309

Horse-chestnut
40–60'
pg. 315

Kentucky Coffeetree
40–60'
pg. 311

Laurel Oak
40–60'
pg. 123

Loblolly Bay
40–60'
pg. 187

Norway Maple
40–60'
pg. 217

Overcup Oak
40–60'
pg. 251

Paper Birch
40–60'
pg. 97

Pond Cypress
40–60'
pg. 5

Red Maple
40–60'
pg. 207

Redbay
40–60'
pg. 179

River Birch
40–60'
pg. 93

Shagbark Hickory
40–60'
pg. 287

Southern Sugar Maple
40–60'
pg. 205

**Swamp
White Oak**
40–60'
pg. 239

White Ash
40–60'
pg. 261

White Poplar
40–60'
pg. 219

White Spruce
40–60'
pg. 11

Black Maple
40–70'
pg. 211

Pond Pine
40–70'
pg. 43

Quaking Aspen
40–70'
pg. 83

Tamarack
40–70'
pg. 51

**Mockernut
Hickory**
40–80'
pg. 289

**Northern
Catalpa**
40–80'
pg. 73

Red Pine
40–80'
pg. 35

Weeping Willow
40–80'
pg. 109

Green Ash
50–60'
pg. 265

Shingle Oak
50–60'
pg. 125

**American
Basswood**
50–70'
pg. 191

**Atlantic
Whitecedar**
50–70'
pg. 57

Bigtooth Aspen
50–70'
pg. 85

Black Tupelo
50–70'
pg. 139

Chinquapin Oak
50–70'
pg. 127

Norway Spruce
50–70'
pg. 19

Pin Oak
50–70'
pg. 231

Pitch Pine
50–70'
pg. 41

Red Oak
50–70'
pg. 247

Red Spruce
50–70'
pg. 15

SILHOUETTE QUICK COMPARES, *continued*

Slippery Elm
50–70'
pg. 81

Sugar Maple
50–70'
pg. 209

Sweet Birch
50–70'
pg. 95

Tree-of-heaven
50–70'
pg. 273

Water Oak
50–70'
pg. 229

White Oak
50–70'
pg. 241

White Willow
50–70'
pg. 111

Yellow Birch
50–70'
pg. 99

Yellow Buckeye
50–70'
pg. 317

Balsam Fir
50–75'
pg. 23

Black Cherry
50–75'
pg. 137

Black Walnut
50–75'
pg. 303

**Swamp
Chestnut Oak**
50–80'
pg. 129

Swamp Tupelo
50–80'
pg. 141

Willow Oak
50–80'
pg. 119

**Bitternut
Hickory**
50–100'
pg. 283

Scarlet Oak
60–70'
pg. 235

American Beech
60–80'
pg. 169

**Lombardy
Poplar**
60–80'
pg. 87

Pumpkin Ash
60–80'
pg. 263

Red Hickory
60–80'
pg. 285

**Southern
Magnolia**
60–80'
pg. 149

**Southern
Red Oak**
60–80'
pg. 249

Sugarberry
60–80'
pg. 107

Swamp Cottonwood
60–80'
pg. 89

American Chestnut
60–90'
pg. 199

Chestnut Oak
60–90'
pg. 131

Shumard Oak
60–90'
pg. 237

Sycamore
60–90'
pg. 193

Nutmeg Hickory
70–80'
pg. 291

Shellleaf Hickory
70–90'
pg. 293

Spruce Pine
70–90'
pg. 31

American Elm
70–100'
pg. 79

Eastern Cottonwood
70–100'
pg. 91

Eastern White Pine
70–100'
pg. 49

Pecan
70–100'
pg. 295

Shortleaf Pine
70–100'
pg. 37

Cherrybark Oak
70–130'
pg. 253

Silver Maple
75–100'
pg. 213

Bald Cypress
80–100'
pg. 3

Loblolly Pine
80–100'
pg. 45

Longleaf Pine
80–100'
pg. 47

Slash Pine
80–100'
pg. 39

Sweetgum
80–100'
pg. 223

Tulip-tree
80–100'
pg. 225

Water Tupelo
80–100'
pg. 143

NEEDLE AND LEAF QUICK COMPARES

To help you differentiate among similar-looking tree species, compare your finds with the following leaf images. For each species, we've also included information about the leaf shape and attachment, which can help quickly point you in the right direction.

Note: Leaf images are not to scale.

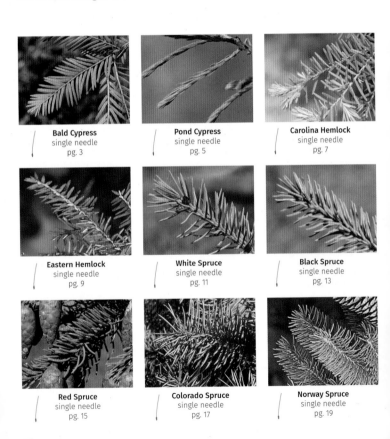

Bald Cypress
single needle
pg. 3

Pond Cypress
single needle
pg. 5

Carolina Hemlock
single needle
pg. 7

Eastern Hemlock
single needle
pg. 9

White Spruce
single needle
pg. 11

Black Spruce
single needle
pg. 13

Red Spruce
single needle
pg. 15

Colorado Spruce
single needle
pg. 17

Norway Spruce
single needle
pg. 19

Fraser Fir
single needle
pg. 21

Balsam Fir
single needle
pg. 23

Table Mountain Pine
clustered needles
pg. 25

Virginia Pine
clustered needles
pg. 27

Scotch Pine
clustered needles
pg. 29

Spruce Pine
clustered needles
pg. 31

Austrian Pine
clustered needles
pg. 33

Red Pine
clustered needles
pg. 35

Shortleaf Pine
clustered needles
pg. 37

Slash Pine
clustered needles
pg. 39

Pitch Pine
clustered needles
pg. 41

Pond Pine
clustered needles
pg. 43

Loblolly Pine
clustered needles
pg. 45

Longleaf Pine
clustered needles
pg. 47

Eastern White Pine
clustered needles
pg. 49

Tamarack
clustered needles
pg. 51

Eastern Redcedar
scaly needles
pg. 53

Eastern Whitecedar
scaly needles
pg. 55

Atlantic Whitecedar
scaly needles
pg. 57

Chinese Privet
simple opposite
pg. 59

European Buckthorn
simple opposite
pg. 61

Eastern Flowering Dogwood
simple opposite
pg. 63

Eastern Wahoo
simple opposite
pg. 65

Buttonbush
simple opposite
pg. 67

Fringetree
simple opposite
pg. 69

Southern Catalpa
simple opposite
pg. 71

Northern Catalpa
simple opposite
pg. 73

Siberian Elm
simple alternate
pg. 75

Winged Elm
simple alternate
pg. 77

American Elm
simple alternate
pg. 79

Slippery Elm
simple alternate
pg. 81

Quaking Aspen
simple alternate
pg. 83

Bigtooth Aspen
simple alternate
pg. 85

Lombardy Poplar
simple alternate
pg. 87

Swamp Cottonwood
simple alternate
pg. 89

Eastern Cottonwood
simple alternate
pg. 91

River Birch
simple alternate
pg. 93

Sweet Birch
simple alternate
pg. 95

Paper Birch
simple alternate
pg. 97

Yellow Birch
simple alternate
pg. 99

Crab Apple
simple alternate
pg. 101

Wild Apple
simple alternate
pg. 103

Hackberry
simple alternate
pg. 105

Sugarberry
simple alternate
pg. 107

Weeping Willow
simple alternate
pg. 109

White Willow
simple alternate
pg. 111

Pussy Willow
simple alternate
pg. 113

Black Willow
simple alternate
pg. 115

Sand Live Oak
simple alternate
pg. 117

Willow Oak
simple alternate
pg. 119

Live Oak
simple alternate
pg. 121

Laurel Oak
simple alternate
pg. 123

Shingle Oak
simple alternate
pg. 125

Chinquapin Oak
simple alternate
pg. 127

Swamp Chestnut Oak
simple alternate
pg. 129

Chestnut Oak
simple alternate
pg. 131

American Plum
simple alternate
pg. 133

Pin Cherry
simple alternate
pg. 135

Black Cherry
simple alternate
pg. 137

Black Tupelo
simple alternate
pg. 139

Swamp Tupelo
simple alternate
pg. 141

Water Tupelo
simple alternate
pg. 143

Sweetbay
simple alternate
pg. 145

Cucumbertree
simple alternate
pg. 147

Southern Magnolia
simple alternate
pg. 149

Ginkgo
simple alternate
pg. 151

Russian-olive
simple alternate
pg. 153

Wax-myrtle
simple alternate
pg. 155

Hawthorn
simple alternate
pg. 157

Juneberry
simple alternate
pg. 159

American Holly
simple alternate
pg. 161

Ironwood
simple alternate
pg. 163

Mountain-laurel
simple alternate
pg. 165

Blue Beech
simple alternate
pg. 167

American Beech
simple alternate
pg. 169

Alternate-leaf Dogwood
simple alternate
pg. 171

Red Mulberry
simple alternate
pg. 173

Eastern Redbud
simple alternate
pg. 175

Carolina Silverbell
simple alternate
pg. 177

Redbay
simple alternate
pg. 179

Common Persimmon
simple alternate
pg. 181

Osage-orange
simple alternate
pg. 183

Witch-hazel
simple alternate
pg. 185

Loblolly Bay
simple alternate
pg. 187

Carolina Basswood
simple alternate
pg. 189

American Basswood
simple alternate
pg. 191

Sycamore
simple alternate
pg. 193

Sourwood
simple alternate
pg. 195

Pawpaw
simple alternate
pg. 197

American Chestnut
simple alternate
pg. 199

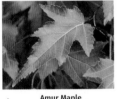

Amur Maple
lobed opposite
pg. 201

Mountain Maple
lobed opposite
pg. 203

Southern Sugar Maple
lobed opposite
pg. 205

Red Maple
lobed opposite
pg. 207

Sugar Maple
lobed opposite
pg. 209

Black Maple
lobed opposite
pg. 211

Silver Maple
lobed opposite
pg. 213

Striped Maple
lobed opposite
pg. 215

Norway Maple
lobed opposite
pg. 217

White Poplar
lobed alternate
pg. 219

Sassafras
lobed alternate
pg. 221

Sweetgum
lobed alternate
pg. 223

Tulip-tree
lobed alternate
pg. 225

Blackjack Oak
lobed alternate
pg. 227

Water Oak
lobed alternate
pg. 229

Pin Oak
lobed alternate
pg. 231

Post Oak
lobed alternate
pg. 233

Scarlet Oak
lobed alternate
pg. 235

Shumard Oak
lobed alternate
pg. 237

Swamp White Oak
lobed alternate
pg. 239

White Oak
lobed alternate
pg. 241

Turkey Oak
lobed alternate
pg. 243

Black Oak
lobed alternate
pg. 245

Red Oak
lobed alternate
pg. 247

Southern Red Oak
lobed alternate
pg. 249

Overcup Oak
lobed alternate
pg. 251

Cherrybark Oak
lobed alternate
pg. 253

Boxelder
compound opposite
pg. 255

American Bladdernut
compound opposite
pg. 257

Carolina Ash
compound opposite
pg. 259

White Ash
compound opposite
pg. 261

Pumpkin Ash
compound opposite
pg. 263

Green Ash
compound opposite
pg. 265

Common Hoptree
compound alternate
pg. 267

Yellowwood
compound alternate
pg. 269

Black Locust
compound alternate
pg. 271

Tree-of-heaven
compound alternate
pg. 273

European Mountain-ash
compound alternate
pg. 275

American Mountain-ash
compound alternate
pg. 277

Common Prickly-ash
compound alternate
pg. 279

Sand Hickory
compound alternate
pg. 281

Bitternut Hickory
compound alternate
pg. 283

Red Hickory
compound alternate
pg. 285

Shagbark Hickory
compound alternate
pg. 287

Mockernut Hickory
compound alternate
pg. 289

Nutmeg Hickory
compound alternate
pg. 291

Shellbark Hickory
compound alternate
pg. 293

Pecan
compound alternate
pg. 295

Poison Sumac
compound alternate
pg. 297

Smooth Sumac
compound alternate
pg. 299

Staghorn Sumac
compound alternate
pg. 301

Black Walnut
compound alternate
pg. 303

Butternut
compound alternate
pg. 305

Water Locust
twice compound
alternate
pg. 307

Honey Locust
twice compound
alternate
pg. 309

Kentucky Coffeetree
twice compound
alternate
pg. 311

Devil's-walkingstick
twice compound
alternate
pg. 313

Horse-chestnut
palmate compound
opposite
pg. 315

Yellow Buckeye
palmate compound
opposite
pg. 317

Ohio Buckeye
palmate compound
opposite
pg. 319

Cabbage Palmetto
palmate compound
alternate
pg. 321

CHAMPION TREES OF THE CAROLINAS

Tall trees have fascinated people for generations. The sheer size and magnitude of a large tree makes us feel good. The following is a list of the champion trees of the Carolinas; a champion tree is the tallest known individual of a given tree species. The list is constantly in flux due to the discovery of previously unknown trees, old trees dying, or trees falling in storms. This is not a complete list of all of Carolinas' tallest trees, but it represents some of the more common largest tree species. For up-to-date information, visit the North Carolina Forest Service web page, which lists all the latest information about champion trees in North Carolina: www.ncforestservice.gov/urban/nc_champion_big_trees_overview.htm. Or visit the page for South Carolina: www.clemson.edu/cafls/departments/fec/champtree/

If the idea of champion trees intrigues you, you can become a tree hunter and join the search for the largest trees in the Carolinas. For more information about how to measure a tree and submit your champion tree candidate, see the above web pages.

Note: Since many of the state record trees are on private property, we have listed only the county in which it is located. Never trespass when attempting to identify a champion tree.

Measurement notes: The height of the tree is in feet. The circumference is measured in inches and measured at 4.5 feet above the ground.

NORTH CAROLINA

TREE	HEIGHT	CIRCUMFERENCE	COUNTY
Eastern White Pine	180'	152"	Jackson
Cherrybark Oak	160'	228"	Northampton
Bitternut Hickory	152'	185"	Jackson
American Sycamore	152'	193"	Nash
Northern Red Oak	150'	222"	Avery
Shumard Oak	151'	231"	Halifax
Eastern Hemlock	159'	192"	Macon
Laurel Oak	147'	194"	Bertie
Eastern Cottonwood	144'	260"	Halifax
Red Spruce	147'	152"	Swain
Pin Oak	145'	206"	Nash

SOUTH CAROLINA

TREE	HEIGHT	CIRCUMFERENCE	COUNTY
Loblolly Pine	170'	181"	Richland
Sweetgum	160'	203"	Richland
Chestnut Oak	155'	132"	Greenville
Eastern White Pine	152'	145"	Oconee
Sand Hickory	151'	134"	Greenville
Shumard Oak	145'	281"	Richland
Eastern Cottonwood	145'	166"	Edgefield
Bitternut Hickory	143'	106"	Richland
Cherrybark Oak	141'	282"	Richland
Tuliptree	134'	253"	Abbeville
Laurel Oak	130'	246"	Richland

mature
fruit

bark

flower

fruit

Common Name
Scientific name

Family: common family name (scientific family name)

Height: average range in feet and meters of the mature tree from ground to top of crown

Tree: overall description; may include a shape, type of trunk, branches, or crown

Leaf/Needle: type of leaf or needle, shape, size, and attachment; may include lobes, leaflets, margin, veins, color, or leafstalk

Bark: color and texture of the trunk; may include inner bark or thorns

Flower: catkin, flower; may include shape, size, or color

Fruit/Cone: seed, nut, berry; may include shape, size, or color

Fall Color: color(s) that deciduous leaves turn to in autumn

Origin/Age: native or non-native to the state; average life span

Habitat: type of soil, places found, sun or shade tolerance

Range: throughout or part of the Carolinas where the tree is found, places where planted

Stan's Notes: Helpful identification information, history, origin, and other interesting gee-whiz nature facts.

Average mature tree compared with a two-story house. Icon is shown on a smaller scale when average tree height is over 50 feet.

Shape of an individual needle, needle cluster, or leaf. Use this icon to compare relative size among similarly shaped leaves.

bark

cone

knees

Bald Cypress
Taxodium distichum

Family: Bald Cypress (Cupressaceae)

Height: 80–100' (24.5–30.5 m)

Tree: large conical tree, enlarged straight trunk with a flared base (buttress), spreading into ridges, wide spreading branches, crown often pointed

Needle: single needle, ½–¾" (1–2 cm) long, in 2 rows on slender green twigs, pointed at the tip, soft and flexible to touch, appearing feather-like, yellowish green above, whitish below

Bark: brown to gray, with narrow fibrous ridges, peeling off in long strips

Cone: green, turning gray to brown when mature, ¾–1" (2–2.5 cm) wide, solitary or in small clusters at the end of branch, several 4-sided woody cone scales

Fall Color: brown

Origin/Age: native; 500–750 years

Habitat: wet soils, swamps, by slow rivers that flood often, can grow in dry upland soils, sun to partial shade

Range: eastern half of the Carolinas

Stan's Notes: Called "Bald" since it's a deciduous conifer, losing its leaves (needles) in fall and growing new ones in spring. Produces a large flaring or fluted base, which helps stabilize it when growing in soft, wet soils. Produces large aboveground or water growths called knees (see inset). A long-lived tree, some are more than 2,000 years old and are among the oldest living things in North America. Often called the Sequoia of the East, reaching over 100 feet (30.5 m) tall and nearly 40 feet (12 m) around at the base. Decay- and insect-resistant wood has been used to build boats and bridges. Its seeds are an important food for wildlife such as ducks and deer.

bark

cone

knees

Pond Cypress
Taxodium ascendens

Family: Bald Cypress (Cupressaceae)

Height: 40–60' (12–18 m)

Tree: medium-sized narrow conical tree, straight trunk, flared base (buttress), many branches, narrow pointed crown

Needle: single needle, 1–2" (2.5–5 cm) long, pressed close to twig, soft and flexible to the touch, feather-like, bright green to yellowish green

Bark: brown to gray, with narrow fibrous ridges, peeling off in long strips

Cone: green, turning gray to brown at maturity, round, ½–1" (1–2.5 cm) wide, solitary or in small clusters at the end of branch

Fall Color: yellow to brown

Origin/Age: native; 500–600 years

Habitat: wide variety of soils, swamps, along slow-moving rivers, dry uplands, partial shade

Range: eastern half of the Carolinas, planted in parks and yards

Stan's Notes: Considered by some as just a smaller variety of Bald Cypress (pg. 3), but is a separate species. Leaves (needles) point toward the end of a twig, while the needles of the Bald Cypress are in two horizontal rows. Wide or flared buttress helps stabilize tree when growing in soft wet soils. Has knees (see inset) similar to Bald Cypress, but not as many. Doesn't grow knees in dry habitats. Often planted along streets and other dry sites, as roots do little damage to roads and sidewalks. Grows in just about any soil. Tolerates drought by shedding its needles and growing new ones when drought is over. Can be very long lived, with many trees living over 500 years.

bark

cone

Carolina Hemlock
Tsuga caroliniana

Family: Pine (Pinaceae)

Height: 40–60' (12–18 m)

Tree: pyramid shape, spreading branches are horizontal, often with drooping tips, stout pointed crown

Needle: single needle, ¼–¾" (.6–2 cm) long, spreading in all directions from a flexible twig, soft, flat and flexible, tiny notch at the tip, shiny dark green above, lighter-colored with 2 whitish lengthwise parallel lines below

Bark: dark brown to reddish brown, deeply furrowed with broad flat-topped ridges

Cone: green, turning brown at maturity, round to ovate, 1–1½" (2.5–4 cm) long, on a short stalk, at the end of twig, hanging down

Origin/Age: native; 150–200 years

Habitat: dry upland soils, mixed forests, rocky slopes and ledges in the higher elevations of the Appalachian Mountains, sun

Range: western quarter of the Carolinas, planted in parks and yards

Stan's Notes: Differentiated from the Eastern Hemlock (pg. 9) by its larger cones and its needles, which extend in all directions from the twigs. Seed production begins at about 20 years and heavy seed crops are achieved at 25–30 years. Many birds eat seeds that fall from the cones. Pure stands of this tree provide shelter for birds and mammals during inclement weather. Many cultivated varieties are planted as ornamentals throughout the Carolinas for their attractive shape and size.

bark

cone

Eastern Hemlock
Tsuga canadensis

Family: Pine (Pinaceae)

Height: 40–60' (12–18 m)

Tree: pyramid shape, spreading branches are horizontal with drooping tips, irregular crown

Needle: single needle, ½–1" (1–2.5 cm) long, arranged in 2 rows with a few shorter needles on the upper row, borne on a flexible tan twig, soft, flat and flexible, tapering at the end, dark yellow-green above, lighter-colored with 2 whitish lengthwise parallel lines below

Bark: dark brown to dark gray in color, deeply grooved with broad flat-topped ridges

Cone: green, turning brown at maturity, round to ovate, ½–1" (1–2.5 cm) long, on a short stalk, at the end of twig, hanging down

Origin/Age: native; 150–200 years (some reach 600 years)

Habitat: wet soils, cool moist sites, shade tolerant

Range: western quarter of the Carolinas, planted in parks and yards

Stan's Notes: One of four species of hemlock in the U.S. An extremely long-lived tree, some with trunk diameters measuring 4 feet (1.2 m). A very shade-tolerant tree, often growing in dense shade of taller trees, growing slowly until reaching the canopy. Because the tip of the leader shoot (treetop) droops, it often doesn't grow as straight as the other conifers. Bark is rich in tannic acid (tannin) and was once used to tan hides. Open cones will remain on the tree for up to two years. Has heavy seed crops every 2–3 years. Doesn't reproduce very well, as young trees are fragile and often do not reach maturity. Doesn't transplant well. Also called Canada Hemlock.

bark

cone

close-up

White Spruce
Picea glauca

Family: Pine (Pinaceae)

Height: 40–60' (12–18 m)

Tree: single straight trunk, many horizontal branches sometimes sloping down, ragged conical crown

Needle: single needle, ⅓–¾" (.8–2 cm) long, stiff, pointed, square in cross section, aromatic when crushed, bluish green with a line of white dots on all sides

Bark: light gray in color, many flaky scales, inner bark is salmon pink

Cone: green, turning brown at maturity, smooth to the touch, 1–2½" (2.5–6 cm) long, single or in clusters, hanging from branch

Origin/Age: non-native; 175–200 years

Habitat: variety of soils, often grows on banks of lakes and streams, sometimes in pure stands, sun to partial shade

Range: planted in parks, yards and along streets

Stan's Notes: Also known as Skunk Spruce because its crushed needles give off a strong odor that reminds some of skunk. Needles have a whitish cast, giving this tree its common name. Like all other species of spruce, White Spruce needles are square in cross section. Needles often last 7–10 years before falling off, leaving a raised base on the twig. Susceptible to fire and Spruce Budworm, a caterpillar that eats new needles. Lower branches die and fall off, leaving the trunk straight and lacking branches. A variety, Black Hills White Spruce (*P. glauca* var. *densata*), is a widely planted urban tree.

bark

cone

Black Spruce
Picea mariana

Family: Pine (Pinaceae)

Height: 25–50' (7.5–15 m)

Tree: small to medium-sized slender tree with a narrow pyramid shape, many dead lower branches, upper branches widely spread and drooping

Needle: single needle, ¼–1" (.6–2.5 cm) long, densely set along twig, straight, blunt-tipped, square in cross section, dull blue-green

Bark: reddish brown in color, large scales, inner bark is olive green

Cone: lavender to purple, turning brown when mature, egg-shaped (ovate), ½–1½" (1–4 cm) long, hanging from the branch

Origin/Age: non-native; 150–200 years

Habitat: wet or poorly drained soils, bogs, peats, often in pure stands or with Tamarack (pg. 51)

Range: planted in parks and yards

Stan's Notes: A relatively slow-growing, long-lived tree, it is one of seven spruce species native to North America. Common along bogs and marshes, with cones usually occurring at the top of the tree. Cones mature in autumn but often don't open, remaining on the tree for up to 15 years. Heat from fire opens the cones, after which many seeds are released. This species can live as long as 200 years, but obtains a height of only 50 feet (15 m). Young twigs have tiny orange-to-brown hairs. Treetops are commonly used in planters in winter for decoration. Long fibers in the wood make it desirable for making paper. A golden-colored pitch that collects on wounds was once gathered and sold as spruce gum. Differentiated from Red Spruce (pg. 15) by its smaller cones and very different habitat.

immature
cone

bark

cone

Red Spruce
Picea rubens

Family: Pine (Pinaceae)

Height: 50–70' (15–21 m)

Tree: medium tree, single straight trunk, broadest at the bottom, narrow pointed top

Needle: single needle, ½–¾" (1–2 cm) long, stout, stiff, pointed tip, 4-sided (square in cross section), shiny yellow-green with white stripes

Bark: reddish brown, thin with many small scales

Cone: green (sometimes purplish), turns reddish brown at maturity, leathery, cylindrical, 1¼–2" (3–5 cm) long, tapers to a round tip, hanging from branch, stalk-less, round cone scales, many winged seeds within, falls apart in autumn

Origin/Age: native to North Carolina, non-native to South Carolina; 300–400 years

Habitat: rocky soils on steep slopes, ridges and mountains up to 5,500 feet (1,680 m), acid soils, moist soils

Range: western tip of North Carolina, planted throughout the Carolinas in parks and yards

Stan's Notes: The southernmost spruce in the eastern U.S. Often in pure stands. Favors nutrient-poor soils. A shallow-rooted tree, falling victim to windstorms. Can thrive in deep shade for many years, but grows nearly twice as fast in full sun. An extremely important commercial tree species. Wood is straight grained, strong, lightweight and used to make musical instruments, lumber and paper. Spruce gum was once used as raw material for chewing gum, and twigs and needles were used with flavoring and sugar to make spruce beer. Starts producing cones and seeds at 20–30 years, but maximum production occurs later. Has very large seed crops every 4–6 years. Also called Yellow Spruce or Eastern Spruce.

bark

cone

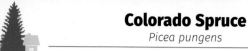

Colorado Spruce
Picea pungens

SINGLE NEEDLE

Family: Pine (Pinaceae)

Height: 40–60' (12–18 m)

Tree: pyramid shape, lower branches are the widest and often touch the ground

Needle: single needle, ½–1" (1–2.5 cm) long, very stiff, very sharp point on the end, square in cross section, bluish green to silvery blue

Bark: grayish brown and flaky, becoming reddish brown and deeply furrowed with age

Cone: straw-colored, 2–4" (5–10 cm) long, in clusters or single, hanging down

Origin/Age: non-native, was introduced to the Carolinas from the Rocky Mountains; 150–200 years (can reach 600 years in some western states)

Habitat: variety of soils, does best in clay and moist soils, sun

Range: planted in cities, parks, along roads, around homes

Stan's Notes: A common Christmas tree and landscaping tree that is widely planted around homes and along city streets. Naturalized now throughout the Carolinas. A victim of the Spruce Budworm and needle fungus, so it's not planted as much anymore. Very susceptible to *Cytospora* canker, which invades stressed trees, causing loss of branches and eventual death. Will grow in a wide variety of soils, but prefers moist and well drained. Slow growing, some living up to 600 years in the West. Needles are very sharp and square in cross section. The species name *pungens* is Latin for "sharp-pointed." Also known as Blue Spruce or Silver Spruce.

cone

bark

Norway Spruce
Picea abies

Family: Pine (Pinaceae)

Height: 50–70' (15–21 m)

Tree: pyramid shape, single trunk, branches drooping or weeping

Needle: single needle, ½–1" (1–2.5 cm) long, with a slight curve, stiff and pointed, square in cross section, aromatic when crushed, deep blue green

Bark: reddish gray, many round scales

Cone: straw brown, papery, 2–7" (5–18 cm) long, hangs from branch

Origin/Age: non-native, introduced to the U.S. from Europe and Asia; 150–200 years

Habitat: rich moist soils, sun

Range: planted as windbreaks, in cemeteries, parks, yards

Stan's Notes: The fastest growing and one of the tallest spruces in the Carolinas, popular for planting as windbreaks. Produces the largest cones of all spruces. Generally a very healthy tree with few diseases. Sometimes has deformed cones, caused by Cooley Spruce Gall Aphids chewing on its new growth. Introduced from Europe, as the common name implies, it is the dominant tree species in the Black Forest area of Germany. One of the earliest trees used for reforestation in North America. The bark on the twigs is orange, turning reddish brown on the small branches. The trunk oozes a pitch known as burgundy pitch, which has been used in varnishes and medicine. Many horticultural varieties of this tree are available.

bark

cone

underside

Fraser Fir
Abies fraseri

Family: Pine (Pinaceae)

Height: 30–40' (9–12 m)

Tree: tapering spire, many horizontal branches from the ground up

Needle: single needle, ½–1" (1–2.5 cm) long, spreading almost at right angles in 2 rows on a slender twig, crowded and curved near the end of twig, flat, shiny dark green above with 2 broad silvery white lines below

Bark: gray to brown, smooth with thin resin blisters (pitch pockets), becoming scaly with age

Cone: dark purple, 1½–2½" (4–6 cm) long, erect on top branches

Origin/Age: native to North Carolina, non-native to South Carolina; 50–100 years

Habitat: poor moist soils, with other conifers, sun

Range: western quarter of North Carolina, planted throughout the Carolinas in parks and yards, becoming a popular tree in landscaping

Stan's Notes: A very popular cut tree during the holidays because of its fragrance and ability to hold its needles for long periods of time. Named after Scottish explorer John Fraser (1750–1811), who first introduced it to many parts of the world. Originally found in the high mountains of North Carolina, Tennessee and Virginia. It is most common in higher elevations of the Appalachian Mountains. Very similar to Balsam Fir (pg. 23) and grows in similar habitats.

bark

cone

Balsam Fir
Abies balsamea

Family: Pine (Pinaceae)

Height: 50–75' (15–23 m)

Tree: tapering spire, many horizontal branches from the ground up

Needle: single needle, ½–1" (1–2.5 cm) long, with a spiral arrangement on the twig, soft, flat, blunt-tipped, shiny green above with 2 silvery lengthwise lines or grooves below

Bark: light gray, smooth with many very aromatic raised resin blisters (pitch pockets), breaking with age and leaving brown scales

Cone: bluish, 2–4" (5–10 cm) long, erect in dense clusters near the top of tree

Origin/Age: non-native; 100–150 years

Habitat: moist soils, in shaded forests, along bogs, sun to partial shade

Range: planted in parks, yards and along streets

Stan's Notes: Well known for its fragrant needles, this is a popular Christmas tree because it holds its needles well after cutting. One of 50 fir species worldwide. One of nine fir species in North America and one of only two species east of the Rocky Mountains, with the Fraser Fir (pg. 21) native to the Appalachian Mountains. Often attacked by the Spruce Budworm, which eats the new needles. The upright cones break apart by autumn, leaving only a thin central stalk. Resin from the trunk was once used for making varnishes and sealing birch bark canoes. The common name "Balsam" comes from the Greek root *balsamon*, which refers to aromatic oily resins found in the tree. Also called Eastern Fir or Canada Balsam.

bark

cone

Table Mountain Pine
Pinus pungens

Family: Pine (Pinaceae)

Height: 20–40' (6–12 m)

Tree: single or multiple crooked trunks, wide irregular crown of horizontal branches

Needle: clustered needles, 2 per cluster, 1¼–2½" (3–6 cm) long, each needle is stout, stiff and slightly twisted, dark green with white stripes

Bark: reddish brown with thin furrows and small scales

Cone: green, turning light brown at maturity, ovate, 2–4" (5–10 cm) long, in clusters of 3–5, often points down toward the trunk, stalkless, cone scales thick and strong, outer edge has a stout curved spine, containing many winged seeds, remaining on the tree many years after opening

Origin/Age: native; 300–400 years

Habitat: dry rocky soils, steep slopes and mountain ridges up to 4,500 feet (1,370 m), sun to partial shade

Range: western half of North Carolina, northwestern corner of South Carolina

Stan's Notes: This species was first collected and named in 1794 near Table Rock Mountain in North Carolina. Grows only (endemic) in the Appalachian Mountains. Also called Mountain Pine, Prickly Pine or Hickory Pine. Known as Squirrel Pine because squirrels pull unopened cones from the tree to get seeds. The species name *pungens* is Latin for "sharp-pointed" and refers to the sharp spines on cones. Often grows as wide as it is tall. Wood is not straight and has many knots, so it doesn't have much commercial value. Used mainly for firewood and pulpwood. Often the first pine to return after an area is logged or burned. A sticky resin in the cone keeps it closed until exposed to heat from forest fires. Some cones will open if the tree is located on warm southern exposures.

immature cone

mature cone

bark

Virginia Pine
Pinus virginiana

Family: Pine (Pinaceae)

Height: 30–60' (9–18 m)

Tree: medium tree, semi-straight trunk, long spreading horizontal branches, irregular round crown

Needle: clustered needles, 2 per cluster, 1½–3" (4–7.5 cm) long, each needle is soft, flexible, slightly twisted and fragrant when crushed, light to dull green

Bark: brown to gray with thin shaggy ridges and flakes

Cone: green, turning reddish brown when mature, egg-shaped, tapers near tip, 1½–2¾" (4–7 cm) long, short stalk, cone scales have a ridge and are tipped with a long prickle, stays on tree for many years

Origin/Age: native; 75–100 years

Habitat: sandy soils, clay, well-drained sites, old fields and abandoned farms, sun

Range: western half of North Carolina, western quarter of South Carolina, planted in parks and yards

Stan's Notes: A medium-size tree, more short-lived than other pines. Usually grows in pure stands with Eastern Redcedar (pg. 53) or other pine species. Often called Poverty Pine or Scrub Pine due to its scrubby, scraggly appearance, a result of the poor soils it inhabits. Frequently used to reforest areas with poor or badly eroded soils. Quickly colonizes recently burned areas and old farm fields. Often planted and sold as a Christmas tree. Noted for its dark green color, pleasant pine scent and retention of needles. Used for pulpwood, firewood and railroad ties. Seldom used in the commercial lumber trade. Favorite of woodpeckers, which excavate nesting cavities in its dead trunks. Its prolific seed source is favored by Pine Siskins and other finches. Deer browse on branches of young trees in winter.

bark

cone

peeling bark

Scotch Pine
Pinus sylvestris

CLUSTERED NEEDLES

Family: Pine (Pinaceae)

Height: 30–80' (9–24.5 m)

Tree: single trunk that is often crooked, with spreading irregular crown

Needle: clustered needles, 2 per cluster, 1½–3" (4–7.5 cm) long, each needle is stiff, twisted and pointed

Bark: orange brown and flaky lower, bright orange and papery upper

Cone: ovate, 1–2½" (2.5–6 cm) long, on a short stalk, in clusters of 2–3, frequently pointing backward up the branch

Origin/Age: non-native, introduced to the U.S. from Europe; 100–150 years

Habitat: well-drained sandy soils, sun

Range: planted along roads, in parks and yards and as shelterbelts

Stan's Notes: One of the more popular Christmas trees grown. Among the first species of trees introduced to North America. The most widely distributed pine in the world, found from Europe to eastern Asia, the Arctic Circle to the Mediterranean Sea, and now North America. In Europe it grows tall and straight, but in North America it seldom has a straight trunk because of the seed source chosen by early settlers; apparently it was easier to collect cones for seeds by climbing trees with crooked trunks. Growing conditions, insect pests and disease also crook trunks. Easily identified by its orange-to-red upper branch bark (see inset) that often peels from the branches in thin papery strips. The main trunk bark has loose scales that fall off to reveal a reddish brown inner bark. Two twisted needles per cluster are characteristic. Also known as Scots Pine.

bark

cone

Spruce Pine
Pinus glabra

Family: Pine (Pinaceae)

Height: 70–90' (21–27.5 m)

Tree: large tree, single trunk, sparse horizontal branches near top, broad round crown

Needle: clustered needles, 2 per cluster, 1–4" (2.5–10 cm) long, each needle is slender and flattened, sometimes twisted, dark green

Bark: gray, thin and smooth when young, becoming furrowed with flat scales and ridges with age

Cone: green, turning reddish brown at maturity, ovate, 1¼–3" (3–7.5 cm) long, nearly stalkless, pointing backward up the branch, each cone scale is flat with a tiny spine at tip

Origin/Age: native; 100–150 years

Habitat: wet soils, low areas with standing water after heavy rains, along rivers, wetlands, partial shade to sun

Range: southern tip of South Carolina, planted in parks and yards

Stan's Notes: A minor tree species in the South, naturally occurring from the southern tip of South Carolina to eastern Texas to northern Florida. Usually not in pure stands, unlike many other pines. Often associated with deciduous trees. Spruce Pine is a good landscape tree for parks and yards because it grows in a variety of soils and is relatively shade tolerant. The wood is brittle and doesn't have much commercial value. Also called Cedar Pine, Walter Pine or Bottom White Pine.

bark

cone

Austrian Pine
Pinus nigra

CLUSTERED NEEDLES

Family: Pine (Pinaceae)

Height: 40–60' (12–18 m)

Tree: often irregular-shaped with large, open horizontal branches, broad round crown

Needle: clustered needles, 2 per cluster, 3–6" (7.5–15 cm) long, each needle is twisted, sharply pointed, not breaking cleanly when bent, dark green

Bark: gray brown with reddish branches, very scaly

Cone: green, turning brown at maturity, woody, ovate, 1–3" (2.5–7.5 cm) long, each cone scale ending in a sharp point

Origin/Age: non-native, introduced to the U.S. from southern Europe; 100 or more years

Habitat: wide variety of soils, sun, shade

Range: planted in parks, along roads, as windbreaks and wildlife shelterbelts

Stan's Notes: A very important tree, also known as European Black Pine. Originally from Europe, it was introduced to North America in 1759. This was the first species of trees to be planted during the dedication of the Dust Bowl Shelterbelt Project in 1935. Frequently confused with Red Pine (pg. 35) but easily differentiated from it by the way the needles break. Unlike Red Pine needles, Austrian Pine needles don't break cleanly when bent. Widely planted in parks and along roads because of its tolerance to salt spray, air pollution and dry soils. Easily grown from seed, it thrives in many soil types and transplants well.

immature cone

bark

cone

Red Pine
Pinus resinosa

Family: Pine (Pinaceae)

Height: 40–80' (12–24.5 m)

Tree: single straight trunk, dead lower branches fall off soon after dying, broad round crown

Needle: clustered needles, 2 per cluster, 4–6" (10–15 cm) long, each needle straight, brittle, pointed, breaks when bent, dark green

Bark: reddish brown, becoming redder higher up, many flat scales or plates

Cone: green, turning brown at maturity, 2–3" (5–7.5 cm) long, containing many small brown nutlets

Origin/Age: non-native; 150–200 years

Habitat: dry sandy soils, often in pure stands, sun

Range: frequently in mass plantings, planted in parks, yards and along streets

Stan's Notes: A very impressive sight when planted in large pure stands. Often planted and sold as Christmas trees. Also called Norway Pine because the early settlers confused the tree with the Norway Spruce (pg. 19) of northern Europe. Often confused with Austrian Pine (pg. 33), which has needles as long but that bend without breaking cleanly. Common name comes from its reddish bark. The scaly bark peels off the mature tree and lies at its base, resembling scattered jigsaw puzzle pieces. Branches occur in whorls around the trunk. Cones remain on tree for several years. Heavy seed crops every 4–7 years. Needs a fire to expose mineral soils for seeds to germinate. Used in reforestation projects.

immature
cone

bark

cone

Shortleaf Pine
Pinus echinata

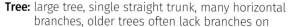

Family: Pine (Pinaceae)

Height: 70–100' (21–30.5 m)

Tree: large tree, single straight trunk, many horizontal branches, older trees often lack branches on lower half, round crown

Needle: clustered needles, 2 or 3 per cluster, 2¾–4½" (7–11 cm) long, each needle is soft, flexible, slender, sharply pointed, yellowish green

Bark: reddish brown with large, irregular flat scales

Cone: yellowish green, turning light brown at maturity, oblong, tapers near tip, 1½–2½" (4–6 cm) long, short stalk, thin cone scale, small prickle at the tip

Origin/Age: native; 100–150 years

Habitat: sandy and gravelly soils on south-facing slopes and ridges, old fields, abandoned farms, sun

Range: throughout

Stan's Notes: One of the fastest-growing pines. After fires or cutting, it quickly reestablishes with many seedlings and suckering shoots, which is uncommon for pines. Often in pure stands or with other pines. Has a hard, strong, yellow-to-orange wood. Is an important commercial tree, producing lumber, millwork, veneer, pulpwood and flooring. Turpentine is produced from the resin. Has the shortest needles of the major southern yellow pines, hence the common name. Wood is often sold as Southern Yellow Pine. Known by other names such as Carolina Pine, Arkansas Pine, Soft Pine and Bull Pine. Reaches cone-bearing maturity at 20–30 years. Seeds look like small maple seeds and are capable of being carried by the wind as far as a quarter mile from the cone. Widespread in the Southeast, it is native in more than 20 states.

bark

cone

Slash Pine
Pinus elliottii

CLUSTERED NEEDLES

Family: Pine (Pinaceae)

Height: 80–100' (24.5–30.5 m)

Tree: large tree with a single trunk, sparse branches, round crown

Needle: clustered needles, 2–3 per cluster, 8–12" (20–30 cm) long, each needle is stout and stiff, glossy dark green

Bark: brown with purplish or orange scaly plates, wide dark furrows

Cone: green, turning shiny dark brown when mature, narrow ovate, 2–6" (5–15 cm) long, nearly stalkless, each cone scale is flat with a short stout spine at tip

Origin/Age: native; 100–200 years

Habitat: wet soils, low areas where water collects after heavy rains, wetlands, sun

Range: southern quarter of South Carolina, planted in parks and yards

Stan's Notes: Usually grows in pure stands in areas too wet for development. Native to South Carolina and planted as far north as North Carolina, Kentucky and Virginia. Also called Florida Slash Pine, Honduras Pine, Yellow Slash Pine, Swamp Pine or Pitch Pine (not to be confused with the Pitch Pine on pg. 41). Endangered Red-cockaded Woodpeckers will nest in cavities of mature (over 60 years old) Slash Pines, and the families will use the cavities year-round. This is extremely unusual behavior compared to other woodpeckers, which use nest cavities only 5–6 weeks to raise their young. Historically, an important tree for lumber.

39

cone

bark

Pitch Pine
Pinus rigida

Family: Pine (Pinaceae)

Height: 50–70' (15–21 m)

Tree: single straight trunk, many horizontal branches with large gaps, broad irregular crown

Needle: clustered needles, 3 per cluster, 3–5" (7.5–12.5 cm) long, each stout, stiff, often twisted, yellow-green

Bark: dark gray to brown, thick and deeply furrowed into broad scales

Cone: yellow brown, turning light brown when mature, egg-shaped, 1¾–2¾" (4.5–7 cm) long, single on branch, stalkless, each scale is thin, flat and armed with a stiff, curved spine, many winged triangular seeds within, remains on branch for many years

Origin/Age: native; 100–150 years

Habitat: sandy and gravelly soils on steep slopes and ridges with elevations up to 3,500 feet (1,070 m)

Range: western quarter of the Carolinas

Stan's Notes: A pine of nutrient-poor soils and dry locations, often growing in small groups. The greatest abundance in North America is in Pennsylvania and New Jersey, where it often forms dense pure stands known as Pine Barrens. Slow growing for the first 5–10 years, then grows rapidly. Cones remain unopened on tree for many years. Forest fires cause them to open and release seeds, which helps to colonize newly burned soils. Often used for reforestation where few other trees will grow or where soil has been depleted. Light brown wood is soft, knotty and not very strong but very resistant to decay and mainly used for fuel and charcoal production. Once used as a resin source for making turpentine and tar. Common name refers to the high resin content. Seeds are an important food source for bird species such as Pine Warbler and chickadee.

bark

cone

Pond Pine
Pinus serotina

Family: Pine (Pinaceae)

Height: 40–70' (12–21 m)

Tree: medium tree with a single straight trunk, sparse irregular crown

Needle: clustered needles, 3 per cluster, 6–8" (15–20 cm) long, each needle is slender, very flexible, slightly twisted, yellowish green

Bark: dark reddish brown, thick with flat plates and wide furrows

Cone: green, turning brown at maturity, round, 2–3" (5–7.5 cm) wide, nearly stalkless, each cone scale ending with a tiny spine at tip, remaining closed for 2 years before opening to release seeds

Origin/Age: native; 100–150 years

Habitat: wet soils, along swamps, bays and other wet places, sun

Range: eastern half of the Carolinas

Stan's Notes: The Carolinas are home to some of the largest Pond Pines. Common name comes from its habit of growing near ponds and other wet places. Also called Marsh Pine, Bay Pine or Pocosin Pine. *Pocosin* is an Algonquin Indian word for "swamp." Species name *serotina* is Latin and means "late," referring to the fact that the cones don't open to release seeds for at least two years or longer. Cones also open and drop seeds due to the heat from forest fires. Often found growing in pure stands because of the massive release of seeds after a fire. Open cones frequently remain on the tree for many years. Sometimes dropped cones become embedded in the branches and give the appearance the branches are growing many cones.

bark

cone

Loblolly Pine
Pinus taeda

Family: Pine (Pinaceae)

Height: 80–100' (24.5–30.5 m)

Tree: large tree, single straight trunk, broad round crown

Needle: clustered needles, 3 per cluster, 6–9" (15–22.5 cm) long, each needle is long, slender, often twisted, green to yellowish green

Bark: black to dark gray when young, becoming reddish brown with scaly ridges with age, resinous and fragrant

Cone: green, turning brown at maturity, ovate, 3–5" (7.5–12.5 cm) long, stalkless, each cone scale is raised with a short stout spine at tip

Origin/Age: native; 100–150 years

Habitat: variety of soils from wet to dry, river bottoms, planted in pure stands, sun

Range: throughout, planted in parks and yards

Stan's Notes: One of the most common pine trees in the Carolinas. A native pine of the southeastern U.S., ranging across more than a dozen states. Common name "Loblolly" means "mud puddle," which accurately describes the wet soils this tree prefers. An extremely fast grower that becomes very tall. Self-pruning tree (lower branches fall off as it grows) that develops a straight trunk, which makes it valuable for lumber. Also planted as a crop tree for pulpwood and lumber and has been introduced to other continents. The most commercially important wild pine species in the Southeast. Several varieties have been developed from this species. Also called Rosemary Pine due to its fragrance, Bull Pine because of its large trunk or Oldfield Pine since it grows in old fields.

bark

cone

Longleaf Pine
Pinus palustris

Family: Pine (Pinaceae)

Height: 80–100' (24.5–30.5 m)

Tree: large tree, single trunk with few branches, open irregular crown

Needle: clustered needles, 3 per cluster, 8–18" (20–45 cm) long, each needle is long, flexible, often twisted, bright green

Bark: orange to brown, thin with scaly plates

Cone: green, turning brown at maturity, cylindrical, 6–10" (15–25 cm) long, nearly stalkless, each cone scale has short stout spine at tip

Origin/Age: native; 100–150 years (some reach over 400 years)

Habitat: dry sandy soils, often in pure stands, sun

Range: eastern half of the Carolinas, planted in parks and yards

Stan's Notes: The state tree of North Carolina. Longleaf Pine can be a long-lived tree, with several in the Carolinas living over 400 years. During the years prior to settlement, these pines may have occupied as many as 60 million acres (24 million ha), but by 1985 less than 4 million acres (1.6 million ha) remained. Old-growth Longleaf Pines are one of the preferred habitats of the endangered Red-cockaded Woodpecker, which nests in cavities excavated in the trunks of living pines. The rarity of old-growth stands is the primary reason for the decline of this woodpecker. An extremely valuable commercial tree, yielding some of the best lumber. Turpentine is produced from the resin. Also known as Georgia Pine, Yellow Pine, Southern Yellow Pine or Longstraw Pine.

bark

immature cone

cone

Eastern White Pine
Pinus strobus

Family: Pine (Pinaceae)

Height: 70–100' (21–30.5 m)

Tree: single tall trunk, whorls of horizontal branching evenly spaced along trunk with branches concentrating near the top when mature, irregular crown

Needle: clustered needles, 5 per cluster, 3–5" (7.5–12.5 cm) long, each needle is soft, flexible and triangular in cross section

Bark: gray to brown and smooth when young, breaking with age into large broad scales that are separated by deep furrows

Cone: green, turning brown when mature, drooping and curved, 4–8" (10–20 cm) long, pointed white tip on each cone scale, resin-coated

Origin/Age: native; 200–250 years

Habitat: wide variety of soils, from dry and sandy to moist upland sites, sun

Range: western quarter of the Carolinas, planted in parks and yards

Stan's Notes: One of the largest trees in the Carolinas. A favorite place for Bald Eagles to build their nests. Also known as Northern White Pine, Soft Pine or Weymouth Pine. The most important tree until about 1890 in North America, where its wood was used in buildings in many large eastern U.S. cities. White pine blister rust, a fungus that slowly girdles the trunk, kills many Eastern White Pines. Restoration efforts are underway in many parts of the country to bring this species back.

bark

cone

Tamarack
Larix laricina

Family: Pine (Pinaceae)

Height: 40–70' (12–21 m)

Tree: cone shape, single straight trunk, narrow crown

Needle: clustered needles on any twigs and branches older than 1 year, 12–30 per cluster, ¾–1¼" (2–3 cm) long, single needles on current year's growth, each needle is soft, pointed, triangular in cross section, light green

Bark: gray when young, reddish brown and flaky scales with age

Cone: light brown, round, ½–1" (1–2.5 cm) diameter, on a short curved stalk

Fall Color: bright golden yellow

Origin/Age: non-native; 100–150 years

Habitat: wet soils, swamps, bogs, occasionally in uplands, sun

Range: planted in parks and yards

Stan's Notes: Like the Bald Cypress (pg. 3) and the Pond Cypress (pg. 5), this is a deciduous conifer. A highly unusual species because it sheds its leaves (needles) in autumn. Turns bright golden yellow in the fall before shedding its needles. One of the northernmost trees in North America and also the world. Almost always grows in wetlands, but can also be planted as an ornamental in yards. Also known as Eastern Larch or American Larch. Larch Sawfly larvae eat the needles and in some years can defoliate entire stands of Tamarack. The roots of this tree have been used for lashing wooden slats together.

cone

bark

Eastern Redcedar
Juniperus virginiana

Family: Cypress (Cupressaceae)

Height: 25–50' (7.5–15 m)

Tree: pyramid shape, single trunk is frequently crooked or leaning and often fluted with folds and creases, may be divided, with pointed crown

Needle: scaly needles, 1–2" (2.5–5 cm) long, made of scale-like needles, ⅛" (.3 cm) long, that overlap each other, each with a sharply pointed tip, dark green

Bark: reddish brown to gray, thin and fibrous, peeling with age into long narrow shreds; reddish inner bark is smooth

Cone: dark blue with a white powdery film, appearing berry-like, ½" (1 cm) long, containing 1–2 seeds

Fall Color: reddish brown during winter

Origin/Age: native; 300 years

Habitat: dry soils, open hillsides, wet swampy areas, sun

Range: western half of the Carolinas, planted in parks and yards

Stan's Notes: One of the first trees to grow back in fields after a fire. Slow growing, producing what appear to be blue berries, which are actually cones. Cones are used to flavor gin during the distillation process. Many bird species spread seeds by eating cones, dispersing seeds in their droppings. Redcedar wood is aromatic and lightweight. Often used to make storage chests, lending its scent to linens. The smooth reddish inner bark was called baton rouge or red stick by early French settlers who found the tree growing in Louisiana. Affected by cedar-apple rust, which causes large jelly-like orange growths. Its sharply pointed leaves can cause slight skin irritation. Also called Eastern Juniper or Red Juniper.

mature
cone

immature
cone

bark

Eastern Whitecedar
Thuja occidentalis

Family: Cypress (Cupressaceae)

Height: 30–50' (9–15 m)

Tree: pyramid shape, single or multiple trunks are often crooked or twisted, blunt or pointed dense crown

Needle: scaly needles, 1–2" (2.5–5 cm) long, made of scale-like needles, ¼" (.6 cm) long, that overlap each other, each scale-like needle is soft, with a rounded tip, flat in cross section, light green

Bark: gray and fibrous with shallow furrows, peeling in long strips

Cone: green, turning bluish purple with a white dust-like coating, then light brown at maturity, ½" (1 cm) long, upright in clusters, containing 2 tiny winged nutlets (seeds)

Origin/Age: native; 150–200 years (some reach 800 years)

Habitat: moist or wet soils, often in pure stands, higher elevations of the Appalachian Mountains

Range: western two-thirds of the Carolinas, planted in parks and yards

Stan's Notes: A common tree of bogs and swamps, and favorite food of deer during winter. Slow growing but with a very long life, with some trees over 700 years old. Also known as Northern Whitecedar, Eastern Thuja or Eastern Arborvitae. The common name "Arborvitae," meaning "tree of life," may have come from French voyagers who used white-cedar to treat scurvy, a disease resulting from a lack of vitamin C. The lightweight wood was once used for canoe frames. One of only two species of *Thuja* in North America, it was introduced into Europe by the mid-1500s. More than 100 different varieties are now known for this tree.

cone

bark

Atlantic White-Cedar
Chamaecyparis thyoides

Family: Cypress (Cupressaceae)

Height: 50–70' (15–21 m)

Tree: pyramid shape, single straight trunk, horizontal branches start halfway up, narrow pointed crown

Needle: scaly needles, 1–2" (2.5–5 cm) long, made of scale-like needles overlapping each other, each scale-like needle ¼" (.6 cm) long, soft, rounded tip, flat in cross section, dull green

Bark: reddish brown, thin and fibrous with narrow forked connecting ridges, becoming scaly and loose with age

Cone: green, turning bluish purple with a white dust-like coating, then brown and dry at maturity, ¼" (.6 cm) long, 6 cone scales with 1–2 seeds under each scale

Origin/Age: native; 150–200 years (some reach 1,000 years)

Habitat: wet acid soils, swampy forests, sun to shade

Range: eastern half of North Carolina, scattered in western half of South Carolina, planted in parks and yards

Stan's Notes: A slow-growing to moderate slow-growth evergreen that may live as long as 1,000 years. Begins to flower at 10 years. Flowers each spring, with cones maturing the same year. Usually found in swamps or wet woodlands with acid soils. Often forms pure stands. Found only in a belt along the Atlantic coastal plain from Maine to northern Florida. A favorite food of White-tailed Deer. Many species of birds nest among its branches. The wood from this tree was used for log cabins, roof shingles, barrels and boats. Logs that were submerged in swamps for centuries have been recovered in excellent condition and are still suitable for use as lumber. This tree has been cultivated and is very hardy.

mature
fruit

immature fruit

bark

flower

Chinese Privet

Ligustrum sinense

Family: Olive (Oleaceae)

Height: 10–20' (3–6 m)

Tree: small tree to large shrub, multiple thin trunks, well-branched dense round crown

Leaf: simple, oval to elliptical, 1–2½" (2.5–6 cm) long, oppositely attached, leaves often appear to grow in 2 rows, toothless margin, semi-evergreen, dull green above, paler below, many fine hairs on leaf undersides and twigs

Bark: gray, smooth

Flower: 4-petaled bell-shaped white flower, ¼" (.6 cm) wide, in clusters, 1–4" (2.5–10 cm) long, abundant clusters, usually broader at base and tapering to a point, at end of branch, sweet fragrance

Fruit: fleshy, green berry-like fruit (drupe), turning dark blue to purple at maturity, round, ¼" (.6 cm) wide, containing 1 hard seed

Fall Color: green to brown

Origin/Age: non-native; 25–50 years

Habitat: dry to damp soils, understory of woodlands, along fencerows and streams, disturbed soils, shade

Range: planted in parks and yards

Stan's Notes: Perhaps the largest invasive, exotic species causing problems in the Carolinas. Introduced from China as an ornamental shrub. Several non-native privet species exist in the Carolinas, but this is the most aggressive and troublesome. Often seen in the understory of moist forests. Almost nothing can grow beneath it since the area is so densely shaded. Its berries are eaten by many bird species, which deposit the seeds across the region.

thorn

bark

flower

fruit

European Buckthorn
Rhamnus cathartica

Family: Buckthorn (Rhamnaceae)

Height: 10–20' (3–6 m)

Tree: single or multiple crooked trunks, round crown

Leaf: simple, oval, 1–3" (2.5–7.5 cm) long, oppositely attached, pointed tip, fine-toothed margin, curved and slightly sunken veins, dark green above

Bark: gray, many horizontal white marks (lenticels) and many scales, tiny spine (thorn) in the fork at ends of twigs

Flower: green bell-shaped flower, ¼" (.6 cm) in diameter, in clusters

Fruit: green berry, turning black at maturity, ¼" (.6 cm) in diameter, in clusters, containing 3–4 seeds and remaining on tree throughout winter

Fall Color: green, remaining on tree long after leaves of other trees have dropped

Origin/Age: non-native, introduced from Europe; 25–50 years

Habitat: wide variety of soils, sun to shade

Range: throughout

Stan's Notes: About 100 species of buckthorn trees and shrubs, 12 native to North America. One of two European species that escaped from landscaping. Now naturalized throughout the Carolinas. Grows in thick stands, shading out native plants, making it undesirable. Considered a nuisance, many state and city agencies have programs to eliminate it from parks and woodlands. However, the berries are a consistent food supply for birds, which eat them in large quantities and spread the seeds. Berries are cathartic (cause diarrhea) to humans and can cause severe dehydration. Also called Common Buckthorn.

mature fruit

bark

flower

immature fruit

Eastern Flowering Dogwood
Cornus florida

Family: Dogwood (Cornaceae)

Height: 20–30' (6–9 m)

Tree: small tree with single trunk, spreading horizontal branches, broad flat-topped crown

Leaf: simple, oval to round, 2–5" (5–12.5 cm) in length, oppositely attached, smooth toothless margin, prominent curving veins, medium green above, paler below, and covered with fine hairs

Bark: reddish brown, broken into small square plates

Flower: several tiny green flowers, ½" (1 cm) in length, crowded together and surrounded by 4 creamy white bracts, 1–2" (2.5–5 cm) in length, appearing before the leaves in spring

Fruit: green berry-like fruit (drupe), turning red when mature, ¼–½" (.6–1 cm) diameter, several together on a long fruit stalk, each containing 1–2 seeds

Fall Color: red

Origin/Age: native; 30–50 years

Habitat: moist soils, along forest borders, meadows, shade

Range: throughout, planted in parks and yards

Stan's Notes: Early blooming of showy flowers makes this one of the most beautiful flowering trees in the Carolinas. Fruit is eaten by many bird species. Its hard wood is used to make mallet handles and heads. Red dye was once extracted from the roots. Often planted as an ornamental for its flowers and bright red fall foliage, and as food for wildlife. Because daggers and meat skewers were made from its wood, common name "Daggerwood" may have been slightly changed to "Dogwood."

bark

flower

fruit

Eastern Wahoo
Euonymus atropurpureus

SIMPLE
OPPOSITE

Family: Staff-tree (Celastraceae)

Height: 20–25' (6–7.5 m)

Tree: single or multiple trunks, irregular crown

Leaf: simple, oval, 2–5" (5–12.5 cm) long, oppositely attached, pointed tip, fine-toothed margin, dull green with hairy underside

Bark: greenish gray with reddish brown streaks, smooth

Flower: 4-parted purple flower

Fruit: 4-lobed capsule, turning pink to red at maturity, ½" (1 cm) long, containing 4 seeds

Fall Color: red

Origin/Age: native; 25–50 years

Habitat: moist soils, usually is found along streams, rivers and floodplains, partial shade

Range: scattered in isolated locations throughout western North Carolina, planted in parks and yards

Stan's Notes: Also called Spindle Tree or Burning-bush Euonymus. This is the only *Euonymus* tree species that is native to North Carolina. The pinkish capsules each contain four seeds, which have a fleshy covering. Capsules stay on the tree into winter, with the fleshy fruit and seeds providing a good food source for birds. Seeds are spread by birds. Twigs have distinctive corky ridges or wings. Over 130 species in the world, nearly all in Asia, with one tree and four shrub species in North America. Several of the shrubby *Euonymus* species that were introduced are also called Burning-bush.

bark

flower

fruit

Buttonbush
Cephalanthus occidentalis

Family: Madder (Rubiaceae)

Height: 10–20' (3–6 m)

Tree: small tree with many crooked trunks and slender, vertically spreading branches, irregular crown

Leaf: simple, oval, 2–6" (5–15 cm) long, often opposite but can be in whorls of 3, pointed at tip, round at base, wavy toothless margin, semi-evergreen, shiny green above, paler below, sometimes covered with fine hairs

Bark: gray to brown, deeply furrowed with scaly ridges

Flower: many small white flowers, each ½–¾" (1–2 cm) long, in balls, 1–1½" (2.5–4 cm) wide, on stalks

Fruit: round green aggregate of many small nutlets, turning brown at maturity, ¾–1" (2–2.5 cm) wide, on a long fruit stalk

Fall Color: brown, but can be green

Origin/Age: native; 10–20 years

Habitat: moist soils, along streams and lakes, floodplains, wet meadows, shade

Range: throughout

Stan's Notes: A lowland species found growing in wet areas. Often in association with other lowland tree species such as cottonwood and willow. Sometimes in dense pure stands, usually on lakeshores. The dense stands often make good cover for nesting birds. A fast-growing, short-lived semi-evergreen with attractive flower balls. Also known as Honey-balls or Globe-flowers. Produces large quantities of nutlets, which mature in fall and are eaten by wildlife such as ducks, deer and turkeys. Foliage and bark are poisonous and have been used in folk medicine, but the effectiveness is highly doubtful.

bark

Fringetree
Chionanthus virginicus

Family: Olive (Oleaceae)

Height: 20–40' (6–12 m)

Tree: small to medium tree with short main trunks that branch into many vertically ascending stems, broad round crown

Leaf: simple, 4–8" (10–20 cm) long, oppositely attached, narrowly elliptical, toothless, dark green above, paler below and sometimes covered with tiny hairs, short purplish leafstalk (petiole)

Bark: brown, thin with reddish brown scales

Flower: thin white flower with tiny purple dots, 1" (2.5 cm) long, in hanging clusters, 4–8" (10–20 cm) long, fragrant scent

Fruit: green berry-like fruit (drupe), turning nearly black when mature, ovate, ½–¾" (1–2 cm) wide

Fall Color: yellow

Origin/Age: native; 50–75 years

Habitat: moist soils, river valleys, understory of deciduous forests, shade tolerant

Range: throughout, planted in parks and yards

Stan's Notes: Widely planted as an ornamental tree. Shade tolerant, it does well in moist soils in the shade of larger trees. One of the last trees to produce leaves each spring, appearing dead until its flowers emerge. The genus name *Chionanthus* is Latin for "snow flower" and refers to the flower color. Sometimes called Old Man's Beard because its thin flowers appear like the white hair of an elderly gentleman.

bark

flower

fruit

Southern Catalpa
Catalpa bignonioides

Family: Trumpet-Creeper (Bignoniaceae)

Height: 30–50' (9–15 m)

Tree: medium tree, single short trunk, broad open crown

Leaf: simple, oval to heart-shaped, 4–8" (10–20 cm) long, oppositely attached or whorls of 3 leaves, smooth margin, dull green

Bark: light brown with deep furrows, flat-topped ridges

Flower: large and showy orchid-like flower, cream to white with yellow and purple spots and stripes, 1–2" (2.5–5 cm) long, in clusters, 4–6" (10–15 cm) wide, fragrant scent

Fruit: long bean-like green capsule, turning brown at maturity, 7–16" (18–40 cm) long, splitting open into 2 parts, containing winged seeds

Fall Color: yellow, turning black

Origin/Age: non-native; 40–50 years

Habitat: moist soils, sun to partial shade

Range: planted in parks and yards

Stan's Notes: The large leaves and flowers make this a distinctive tree and a favorite as an ornamental or for shade. Hoards of hungry caterpillars often strip the leaves from the tree, but the foliage is quickly replaced when the caterpillars move on. This can happen several times in a season. Also called Worm Tree or Fish Bait Tree since these caterpillars are used for fish bait. A native tree of the southern states and introduced widely in the U.S. Now naturalized as far north as Illinois and Pennsylvania.

bark

flower

fruit

Northern Catalpa
Catalpa speciosa

Family: Trumpet-Creeper (Bignoniaceae)

Height: 40–80' (12–24 m)

Tree: single trunk, large round crown

Leaf: simple, heart-shaped, 6–12" (15–30 cm) in length, oppositely attached or whorls of 3 leaves, margin lacking teeth, dull green

Bark: light brown with deep furrows, flat-topped ridges

Flower: large, showy orchid-like flower is cream to white with yellow and purple spots and stripes, 2–3" (5–7.5 cm) long, in clusters, 5–8" (13–20 cm) wide, fragrant odor

Fruit: long bean-like green capsule, turning to brown at maturity, 8–18" (20–45 cm) long, splitting open into 2 parts, containing winged seeds

Fall Color: yellow-green, turning black

Origin/Age: non-native, was introduced to the state from the central Mississippi Valley; 40–50 years

Habitat: rich moist soils

Range: in parks and backyards throughout the state, old homesites

Stan's Notes: Catalpa tree leaves are among the largest leaves in the state. There are about a dozen catalpa species, two native to North America. This is a non-native tree that has been successfully planted along streets and boulevards in just about every city in the Carolinas. "Catalpa" is an American Indian name for this tree, but it is also called Catawba, Cigar Tree, or Indian Bean, which all refer to the large seedpods (fruit). Its large showy flowers bloom in spring and attract many insects. Twigs have a soft white pith. Northern is hardier than Southern (pg. 71), which blooms later and has smaller flowers.

fruit

bark

Siberian Elm
Ulmus pumila

Family: Elm (Ulmaceae)

Height: 30–50' (9–15 m)

Tree: single trunk, open irregular crown

Leaf: simple, narrow, ¾–2" (2–5 cm) in length, alternately attached, with pointed tip, asymmetrical leaf base, double-toothed margin, dark green

Bark: gray with rough scales

Fruit: flat green disk (samara), lacking hair when young, turning papery brown when mature, ½" (1 cm) diameter, with a closed notch opposite fruit stalk

Fall Color: yellow

Origin/Age: non-native, introduced from Asia; 50–75 years

Habitat: wide variety of soils, sun

Range: planted in parks and yards, as hedges, around old homesites

Stan's Notes: A small non-native species that was introduced from Asia, with some of the smallest leaves of any of the elm trees. Fast growing but does not attain the height or reach the age of American Elm (pg. 79). Species name *pumila* means "small" and refers to the small stature. Also called Chinese Elm. Chinese Elm (*U. parvifolia*), however, is a different, cultivated species. Thrives in a wide variety of soils and tolerates harsh conditions. Somewhat resistant to Dutch elm disease, often taking much longer to die from the disease than the American Elm, which usually dies quickly.

bark

fruit

winged twig

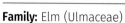

Winged Elm
Ulmus alata

Family: Elm (Ulmaceae)

Height: 30–50' (9–15 m)

Tree: medium tree, single short trunk, lower branches sweep to the ground, wing-like projections on opposite sides of each branch and twig, open round crown

Leaf: simple, oval, 1½–3½" (4–9 cm) long, alternately attached, asymmetrical leaf base, double-toothed margin, pointed tip, slightly rough, thick and firm, dark green above, paler with grayish hairs below

Bark: dark gray, deeply furrowed with flat ridges, corky and scaly

Flower: tiny reddish flower, ¼" (.6 cm) wide, in clusters, 1" (2.5 cm) wide

Fruit: flat, fuzzy green disk (samara), turning reddish at maturity, oval, ¼" (.6 cm) wide, notched tip opposite the fruit stalk, long silver hairs along margin

Fall Color: yellow

Origin/Age: native; 50–100 years

Habitat: wide variety of soils, from wet to dry and sandy to clay, sun to partial shade

Range: throughout, planted in parks and yards

Stan's Notes: Easy to identify by corky winged branches and twigs (see inset), but size of the wings can be highly variable. Found in varied habitats from wet river valleys to dry rocky outcroppings. Popular for planting since so adaptable. Sturdy tree that grows well in urban areas such as along streets. Susceptible to Dutch elm disease. Also called Cork Elm or Wahoo (not Eastern Wahoo on pg. 65).

bark

flower

fruit

American Elm
Ulmus americana

Family: Elm (Ulmaceae)

Height: 70–100' (21–30.5 m)

Tree: one of the tallest of trees, single trunk, prominent root flares, upper limbs fan out gracefully, forming an upright vase shape, branch tips often drooping

Leaf: simple, oval, 3–6" (7.5–15 cm) in length, alternately attached, with pointed tip, asymmetrical leaf base, double-toothed margin, slightly rough to touch, only 2–3 forked veins per leaf

Bark: dark gray, deeply furrowed with flat ridges, corky, sometimes scaly

Flower: tiny reddish brown flower, ¼" (.6 cm) diameter, in clusters, 1" (2.5 cm) wide

Fruit: flat, fuzzy green disk (samara), turning tan when mature, round to oval, ½" (1 cm) diameter, with a notch opposite the fruit stalk

Fall Color: yellow

Origin/Age: native; 150–200 years

Habitat: moist soils, full sun

Range: throughout, planted along city streets, parkways

Stan's Notes: Also called White Elm, this once dominant tree lined just about every city street in eastern North America. Nearly eliminated due to Dutch elm disease, which is caused by a fungus that attacks the tree's vascular system. The fungus was introduced to the U.S. in the 1920s by infected elm logs from Europe. Its arching branches form a canopy, providing shade. The distinct vase shape of the mature tree makes it easy to recognize from a distance. Several Dutch elm disease-resistant trees are now sold at nurseries.

bark

fruit

Slippery Elm
Ulmus rubra

SIMPLE
ALTERNATE

Family: Elm (Ulmaceae)

Height: 50–70' (15–21 m)

Tree: single trunk is divided high, ascending branches, broad flat-topped crown

Leaf: simple, oval, 4–7" (10–18 cm) in length, alternately attached, widest above the middle, asymmetrical leaf base, approximately 26–30 veins with some forked near margin, rough and dark green above, paler below, short leafstalk

Bark: brown to reddish brown, shallow furrows, vertical irregular flat scales, inner bark reddish

Fruit: green disk (samara), turning brown when mature, nearly round, ½–¾" (1–2 cm) in diameter, with a slightly notched tip opposite the fruit stalk, few reddish brown hairs

Fall Color: yellow

Origin/Age: native; 100–125 years

Habitat: rich moist soils, along streams, slopes, sun

Range: throughout, except for the southern tip of South Carolina

Stan's Notes: Due to its habit of growing near water, sometimes is called Water Elm. More often called Red Elm because of its reddish inner bark. The inner bark is fragrant and mucilaginous, hence its common name, "Slippery." Scientific name was formerly *U. fulva*. The inner bark was once chewed to quench thirst and used to cure sore throats. Leaves are smaller than those of most other elm species and feel very rough. Look for some forked veins near the margin. Leaf buds are dark rusty brown and covered with hairs, making this tree easy to identify even without its leaves.

bark

flower

fruit

Quaking Aspen
Populus tremuloides

Family: Willow (Salicaceae)

Height: 40–70' (12–21 m)

Tree: slender tree, straight trunk, lacking any major side branches, round crown

Leaf: simple, nearly round, 1–3" (2.5–7.5 cm) in length, alternately attached, with short sharp point, fine-toothed margin, shiny green above and dull green below, leafstalk (petiole) flattened

Bark: dark gray to brown in color and deeply furrowed lower, greenish white to cream and smooth upper

Flower: catkin, 1–2" (2.5–5 cm) in length, male and female bloom (flower) on separate trees (dioecious) in spring before the leaves bud

Fruit: catkin-like fruit, 4" (10 cm) long, is composed of many tiny green capsules, ⅛" (.3 cm) long, that open and release seeds, seeds are attached to white cottony material and float on the wind

Fall Color: golden yellow

Origin/Age: native to North Carolina, non-native to South Carolina; 60–80 years

Habitat: wet or dry, sandy or rocky soils, sun

Range: western quarter of North Carolina, planted throughout the Carolinas in parks and yards

Stan's Notes: The most widely distributed tree in North America. Common name refers to the leaves, which catch very gentle breezes and shake or quake in the wind. Also known as Trembling Aspen or Popple. Grows in large, often pure stands. Returns from its own roots if cut or toppled. Most reproduce by suckering off their roots, which creates clone trees.

bark

fruit

Bigtooth Aspen
Populus grandidentata

SIMPLE ALTERNATE

Family: Willow (Salicaceae)

Height: 50–70' (15–21 m)

Tree: single trunk with few lower branches and a round irregular crown

Leaf: simple, oval to triangular, 3–6" (7.5–15 cm) long, alternately attached, blunt tip, frequently with 30–34 large saw-like blunt teeth, waxy above, has a long flattened leafstalk

Bark: gray in color with deep furrows and thick ridges lower, pale green to white and smooth upper

Flower: catkin, 4–5" (10–12.5 cm) long

Fruit: catkin-like fruit, 4" (10 cm) long, is composed of many tiny narrow capsules, ⅛" (.3 cm) long, that split open into 2 parts and release cottony seeds

Fall Color: yellow

Origin/Age: native; 50–75 years

Habitat: moist soils, sun

Range: planted throughout the Carolinas in parks and yards

Stan's Notes: One of 35 species of poplar found throughout the northern hemisphere. A fast-growing, short-lived tree. Woolly hairs cover leaves in spring, but by summer they will have turned thick and waxy. Also called Largetooth Aspen, as each leaf often has 30–34 large teeth. Leafstalk (petiole) is flattened and often as long as the leaf. Its large leaves catch the slightest breezes, causing rustling in the same way as the Quaking Aspen (pg. 83). Male and female flowers grow on separate trees (dioecious). Produces heavy seed crops every 3–5 years.

bark

fruit

Lombardy Poplar
Populus nigra

Family: Willow (Salicaceae)

Height: 60–80' (18–24.5 m)

Tree: single straight trunk, ascending branches, narrow columnar crown

Leaf: simple, triangular, 2–4" (5–10 cm) long, alternately attached, often wider than long, pointed tip, fine-toothed margin, dark green above, paler below

Bark: gray with deep furrows lower and smooth upper

Fruit: capsule, ¼" (.6 cm) long, containing many seeds

Fall Color: yellow to brown

Origin/Age: non-native, introduced from Italy; 30–50 years

Habitat: wide variety of soils, sun

Range: planted as windbreaks and as an ornamental in yards and parks

Stan's Notes: A uniquely tall thin tree, usually seen in cities, parks or near older homesteads. Unable to reproduce because all trees planted are males. Often planted in a single row, it was once planted much more than it is planted now. Removed from many city parks because of its non-native status. Fast growing, but short-lived due to its susceptibility to various canker diseases. The species name *nigra* refers to its dark patchy bark. The common name "Lombardy" is also the name of a region in Italy. Known for lining the streets of many Italian cities. Also known as Black Poplar.

bark

fruit

Swamp Cottonwood
Populus heterophylla

Family: Willow (Salicaceae)

Height: 60–80' (18–24.5 m)

Tree: medium to large tree with single or multiple large trunks, few lower branches, narrow round crown

Leaf: simple, oval, 3–6" (7.5–15 cm) long, alternately attached, blunt or rounded tip, fine-toothed margin, dark green above, much paler with many woolly hairs below, long rounded leafstalk

Bark: gray to brown, vertical flat ridges tinged with red

Flower: catkin, 2–3" (5–7.5 cm) long

Fruit: catkin-like fruit, 4" (10 cm) long, is composed of many tiny ovate capsules, ¼" (.6 cm) long, that split open into 2–3 parts and release seeds, seeds are attached to cotton-like filaments and float on the wind

Fall Color: yellow

Origin/Age: native; 50–200 years

Habitat: wet soils, along rivers, floodplains, swamps, sun

Range: eastern half of the Carolinas

Stan's Notes: Closely related to Eastern Cottonwood (pg. 91), which tends to be larger and more common. A fast grower that tolerates soils too wet for other trees. Can survive with its roots covered with standing water. Usually doesn't occur in pure stands. Unlike other *Populus* that have flattened leafstalks, its leafstalks are rounded. Starts to produce seeds at 10 years. Small seeds travel great distances on the wind and even farther on water. However, most reproduction occurs by suckers from stumps and roots. Sometimes called Black Cottonwood, River Cottonwood or Downy Poplar.

bark

flower

seeds

Eastern Cottonwood
Populus deltoides

Family: Willow (Salicaceae)

Height: 70–100' (21–30.5 m)

Tree: large tree with single or multiple trunks, few lower branches and huge, broad irregular crown

Leaf: simple, triangular, 3–6" (7.5–15 cm) in length, alternately attached, coarse-toothed margin, thick and waxy, shiny green above and below, leafstalk long and flattened

Bark: gray with deep flat furrows

Flower: catkin, 2–3" (5–7.5 cm) long

Fruit: catkin-like fruit, 4" (10 cm) long, is composed of many tiny ovate capsules, ¼" (.6 cm) long, that split open into 4 parts and release seeds, seeds (see inset) are attached to cotton-like filaments and float on wind

Fall Color: yellow

Origin/Age: native; 50–200 years

Habitat: wet soils, along streams, rivers and lakes, sun

Range: throughout, planted in wet areas

Stan's Notes: A huge tree of riverbanks, floodplains and other wet areas. Some trees can obtain heights of 150 feet (46 m), with trunk diameters of 7–8 feet (2.1–2.4 m). Fast growing, up to 5 feet (1.5 m) in height and over 1 inch (2.5 cm) in diameter per year. Like many others in its genus, the leafstalks are flat. The species name *deltoides* is Latin, describing the delta-shaped leaf. Known for the massive release of seed-bearing "cotton," hence its common name.

bark

fruit

River Birch
Betula nigra

Family: Birch (Betulaceae)

Height: 40–60' (12–18 m)

Tree: medium-sized tree, single or multiple trunks and spreading irregular crown

Leaf: simple, oval, 2–3" (5–7.5 cm) in length, alternately attached, sometimes with asymmetrical leaf base, double-toothed margin, dark green above, paler green below

Bark: reddish brown to salmon pink, some shaggy curly bark, often flaky, becoming dark and scaly with age

Fruit: many winged nutlets, each ⅛" (.3 cm) wide, in a cone-like seed catkin, 1" (2.5 cm) long

Fall Color: yellow

Origin/Age: native; 50–75 years

Habitat: wet soils, in river valleys, along streams, wetlands and lakes, shade tolerant

Range: throughout, planted in parks and yards

Stan's Notes: This is the southernmost birch tree species in North America, growing as far south as Florida and Texas, and the only birch to disperse its seeds in spring. "River" refers to its habitat near water, where it plays a major role in erosion control. "Birch" comes from the Old German *birka*, meaning "bright," presumably referring to its light bark. The leaves tend to be smaller than the Yellow Birch (pg. 99). Trunk can grow to 1–1½ feet (30–45 cm) wide; often covered with a salmon-pink curled bark. Widely planted as a landscape tree. One of the only native birch resistant to Bronze Birch Borer beetle larvae, which tunnel through inner bark, causing branches or the entire tree to die. Wood is rarely used for any commercial application.

93

fruit

mature bark

Sweet Birch
Betula lenta

Family: Birch (Betulaceae)

Height: 50–70' (15–21 m)

Tree: single straight trunk, round irregular crown

Leaf: simple, oval, 2–3" (5–7.5 cm) in length, alternately attached, with a pointed tip, fine-toothed margin and straight veins with only a few forked near the margin, yellowish green above, lighter below

Bark: brownish red and smooth when young, turning darker with furrows, often becoming scaly

Fruit: many winged nutlets, each ⅛" (.3 cm) wide, in a cone-like seed catkin, ½–1" (1–2.5 cm) long, that grows upright on branch

Fall Color: yellow

Origin/Age: native; 100–150 years

Habitat: rich moist soils, rocky soils, slopes up to 4,000 feet (1,220 m) in the Appalachian Mountains, sun

Range: western quarter of the Carolinas

Stan's Notes: Also called Cherry Birch or Black Birch, both names referring to the color of the bark, which is red and smooth when young but turns dark with age. Fresh twigs that are broken or crushed release a strong scent of wintergreen (methyl salicylate). Very similar to the Yellow Birch (pg. 99), the only major differences being hairy leaf buds and reddish brown bark when older. Can be tapped for sap, which when boiled down makes a syrup. European settlers made birch beer by fermenting the syrup and honey. Resistant to Bronze Birch Borers, which kill most birch species.

bark

fruit

Paper Birch
Betula papyrifera

SIMPLE ALTERNATE

Family: Birch (Betulaceae)

Height: 40–60' (12–18 m)

Tree: single or multiple crooked trunks with drooping branches and open narrow crown

Leaf: simple, oval to triangular, 2–4" (5–10 cm) in length, alternately attached, pointed tip, double-toothed margin, 18 or fewer veins, each ending in a large tooth, dull green above, paler below

Bark: white and smooth with obvious dark horizontal lines (lenticels), often shedding in curled sheets, inner bark reddish

Flower: catkin, 1–2" (2.5–5 cm) long

Fruit: many winged nutlets, each ⅛" (.3 cm) wide, in a cone-like seed catkin, 1–2" (2.5–5 cm) long

Fall Color: yellow

Origin/Age: native; 80–100 years

Habitat: moist or sandy soils, partial to full shade

Range: Appalachian Mountains in northwestern North Carolina, planted as an ornamental tree

Stan's Notes: Also called White Birch or Canoe Birch, both names referring to the white bark that American Indians have long used to construct canoes, baskets and water containers. Dried bark is often used to start campfires. Understory tree that likes moist soil and high humidity. Often doesn't grow well when planted by itself in a sunny suburban lawn. When stressed, trees are attacked by destructive Bronze Birch Borers. Both the male and female flowers are on the same tree (monoecious). Winged nutlets are released from seed catkins in early winter. Found across the northern portion of North America.

immature
fruit

bark

fruit

Yellow Birch
Betula alleghaniensis

Family: Birch (Betulaceae)

Height: 50–70' (15–21 m)

Tree: single trunk with spreading branches and tips that droop, round irregular crown

Leaf: simple, oval to lance-shaped, 3–5" (7.5–12.5 cm) in length, alternately attached, pointed tip, double-toothed margin, dull green

Bark: bronze to yellow in color, thin horizontal marks (lenticels), covered with thin papery scales often curling up in rolls

Flower: catkin, 1–2" (2.5–5 cm) long

Fruit: many winged nutlets, ⅛" (.3 cm) wide, contained in a cone-like seed catkin, 1" (2.5 cm) long, that grows upright on branch

Fall Color: yellow

Origin/Age: native; 100–125 years

Habitat: rich moist soils, often in wet places, partial shade

Range: western quarter of the Carolinas, planted in parks and yards

Stan's Notes: One of the tallest of the birches, often thought to be underutilized in landscaping. Also called Swamp Birch due to its nature of growing in wet areas. Common name Yellow Birch refers to the color of the tree's bark. The bark is very characteristic, making this species one of easier birches to identify. Twigs are aromatic of wintergreen (methyl salicylate) when crushed. A pleasant-tasting tea can be made from the tender twigs. Wood is used to make furniture and veneers. Will produce heavy seed crops every couple of years. Seedlings are heavily browsed by deer.

fruit

bark

flower

Crab Apple
Malus spp.

Family: Rose (Rosaceae)

Height: 10–20' (3–6 m)

Tree: single crooked trunk, broad open crown

Leaf: simple, oval, 2–3" (5–7.5 cm) in length, alternately attached, sometimes with shallow lobes, double-toothed margin, dark green above, lighter-colored and usually smooth or hairless below

Bark: gray, many scales, with 1–2" (2.5–5 cm) long stout thorns often on twigs

Flower: 5-petaled white-to-pink or red flower that is often very showy, 1–2" (2.5–5 cm) wide

Fruit: apple (pome), ranging in color from green and yellow to red, edible, 1–3" (2.5–7.5 cm) diameter, single or in small clusters, hanging from a long fruit stalk well into winter

Fall Color: yellow to red

Origin/Age: native and non-native; 25–50 years

Habitat: wide variety of soils, sun

Range: isolated locations throughout, often around cities or old homesites, planted in yards

Stan's Notes: Many species of cultivated Crab Apple can be found throughout the Carolinas. Others have escaped cultivation and now grow in the wild. Introduced to the U.S. in colonial times. Has since bred with native species, producing hybrids that are hard to identify. Now found throughout the country. Apples are closely related to those sold in grocery stores and have been used in jams and jellies. Cider is often made from the more tart apples. Fruit is an important food source for wildlife. Twigs often have long stout thorns, which are actually modified branches known as spur branches.

bark

flower

fruit

Wild Apple
Malus spp.

SIMPLE ALTERNATE

Family: Rose (Rosaceae)

Height: 10–15' (3–4.5 m)

Tree: single crooked trunk, many spreading branches, creating a broad round crown

Leaf: simple, oval, 2–4" (5–10 cm) in length, blunt-tipped, fine-toothed margin, dark green in color, densely hairy below

Bark: brown, scaly with peeling edges

Flower: 5-petaled showy white (sometimes streaked with pink) flower, 1–2" (2.5–5 cm) wide

Fruit: apple (pome), edible with typical shape and size, 2–4" (5–10 cm) diameter

Fall Color: brown

Origin/Age: native and non-native; 25–50 years

Habitat: dry soils, along fencerows and roadsides, sun

Range: isolated locations throughout, often around cities or old homesites, planted in yards

Stan's Notes: Common apples sold in grocery stores are from trees descended from the Wild Apple. Introduced to the U.S. in colonial times, like many varieties of Crab Apple (pg. 101). The Wild Apple, often associated with former homesteads, is found along roads or fencerows where seedlings were planted or where apples were discarded and seeds have taken root. Some escaped cultivation, and now many varieties are naturalized throughout the country. Wild apples are edible and some are very delicious. The fruit has been used in jellies and desserts, such as pies.

103

immature fruit

bark

flower

fruit

Hackberry
Celtis occidentalis

SIMPLE ALTERNATE

Family: Hemp (Cannabaceae)

Height: 40–60' (12–18 m)

Tree: single trunk, ascending branches with drooping tips, spreading round crown

Leaf: simple, lance-shaped, 2–4" (5–10 cm) long, alternately attached, long tapering tip, asymmetrical leaf base, evenly spaced sharp teeth, hairs on the veins, dark green above, paler below

Bark: unique gray-colored bark is covered with narrow corky ridges, wart-like

Flower: tiny green flower, ⅛" (.3 cm) wide, sprouting from bases of young leaves in early spring

Fruit: green berry-like fruit (drupe), turning deep purple at maturity, sweet and edible when ripe, ¼" (.6 cm) diameter, containing 1 seed

Fall Color: yellow

Origin/Age: native; 100–150 years

Habitat: wide variety of soils, partial shade

Range: western quarter of the Carolinas

Stan's Notes: Unique corky bark makes this tree easy to identify. In fall, mature trees are laden with dark purple berry-like fruit, which typically doesn't last long because it is a favorite food of many bird species. Fruit can remain on the trees throughout winter if not eaten by birds. Commonly found in floodplain forests, but also grows well in drier areas. Suffers from non-fatal witches'-broom—dense clusters of small short twigs at branch ends caused by the combined efforts of a small insect and a fungus. Often has dimple-like galls on leaves (which do not affect the tree's health) caused by mite insects. Also called Northern Hackberry, Sugarberry or Hack-tree.

bark

immature fruit

fruit

Sugarberry
Celtis laevigata

SIMPLE
ALTERNATE

Family: Elm (Ulmaceae)

Height: 60–80' (18–24.5 m)

Tree: single tall straight trunk, slightly drooping lower branches, open round crown

Leaf: simple, lance-shaped, 2–5" (5–12.5 cm) long, alternately attached, long pointed tip often curved, asymmetrical leaf base, toothless to fine-toothed margin, dark green and smooth above, paler below

Bark: light brown to gray or silver, thin and smooth when young, becoming very corky with many warts in an irregular pattern with age

Flower: tiny green flower, ⅛" (.3 cm) wide, sprouting from bases of young leaves in early spring

Fruit: green berry-like fruit (drupe), turning orange red to dark blue upon maturity, sweet and edible when ripe, ¼" (.6 cm) wide, on a long fruit stalk, containing 1 seed

Fall Color: yellow

Origin/Age: native; 100–150 years

Habitat: moist soils, river valleys, usually understory of mixed deciduous trees, sometimes in pure stands, partial shade to sun

Range: throughout, planted in parks and yards

Stan's Notes: Similar to Hackberry (pg. 105), but differentiated by longer, narrower, smoother leaves with toothless margins. Bark has a more irregular pattern of warts and trunk has more smooth open patches than Hackberry. Often planted for its shade, as an accent tree or to attract birds. Birds love to eat the fruit, often stripping the tree of it before it ripens. Also called Sugar Hackberry or Hackberry.

underside

bark

flower

fruit

Weeping Willow
Salix babylonica

Family: Willow (Salicaceae)

Height: 40–80' (12–24.5 m)

Tree: single trunk, often crooked, with many drooping branches often reaching the ground, very broad round crown

Leaf: simple, narrow lance-shaped, 2–4" (5–10 cm) long, alternately attached, pointed tip and fine-toothed margin, bright green above, whitish below

Bark: light brown with many medium furrows and flat-topped corky ridges

Flower: catkin, 1" (2.5 cm) long, standing erect on a short leafy shoot

Fruit: catkin-like fruit, 1" (2.5 cm) long, is composed of many small capsules that open and release seeds, seeds are attached to white cottony material

Fall Color: yellow

Origin/Age: non-native, introduced from Asia; 75–100 years

Habitat: wet or moist soils, sun

Range: planted as an ornamental in parks and yards

Stan's Notes: Also known as Golden Willow because of its yellow twigs and autumn color. Twigs are very flexible and hang nearly to the ground. Many branches break off in heavy winds. Often seen growing along shores of ponds and lakes. Not as commonly planted anymore. An extract from willow bark (salicin) is related to aspirin and was once used in a similar manner. Several tree species have been sold under the name of Weeping Willow, each only slightly different in leaf size or stem color (*S. alba*, *S. pendulina*). Also called Babylon Weeping Willow.

bark

fruit

White Willow

Salix alba

Family: Willow (Salicaceae)

Height: 50–70' (15–21 m)

Tree: medium-sized tree with a large single trunk, open round crown

Leaf: simple, narrow lance-shaped, 2–4" (5–10 cm) long, alternately attached, fine-toothed margin, shiny dark green above, much paler and hairy below, short leafstalk (petiole)

Bark: brown to gray with many narrow flat ridges

Flower: catkin, 1¼–2" (3–5 cm) long, hanging down

Fruit: catkin-like fruit, 2–3" (5–7.5 cm) long, composed of many capsules, ¼" (.6 cm) long, seeds within

Fall Color: yellow

Origin/Age: non-native; 50–75 years

Habitat: wet soils, along rivers and streams, wetlands and other wet places, sun

Range: planted in parks and yards

Stan's Notes: This non-native species was introduced and planted throughout the eastern U.S. so long ago that it is now naturalized in the region and sustains a population on its own. A native of Europe and Asia. Early settlers brought this and other willow species to North America because the bark contains salicin and other chemicals similar to salicylates. Its bark was the original source for aspirin. A tea made from the inner bark reduced fever and relieved arthritis pain or headache. Twigs and bark were used to weave baskets, and wood was used to make tools. Looks similar to Weeping Willow (pg. 109). Also called Basket Willow, Golden Willow or Crack Willow.

fruit

bark

flower

Pussy Willow
Salix discolor

Family: Willow (Salicaceae)

Height: 10–20' (3–6 m)

Tree: small tree, multiple trunks, irregular crown

Leaf: simple, lance-shaped, 2–5" (5–12.5 cm) in length, alternately attached, with shallow irregular teeth, smooth to touch, shiny green above, paler below, lacking hairs, young leaves often reddish and very hairy, 2 small appendages (stipules) on leafstalk

Bark: gray to brown, often red tinges, shallow furrows

Flower: catkin, ½–1" (1–2.5 cm) long, covered with silky hairs when immature, lacking a stalk

Fruit: catkin-like fruit, ½–1" (1–2.5 cm) long, composed of many capsules, ¼" (.6 cm) long, seeds within

Fall Color: yellow

Origin/Age: native; 20–50 years

Habitat: wet soils, along shores, swamps, wetlands, sun

Range: scattered locations throughout the Carolinas, planted as an ornamental shrub or small tree

Stan's Notes: This is one of the best-known willows in the Carolinas. The immature catkins, which are covered with silky hairs known as pussy fur, are often collected and used in floral arrangements in early spring. Twigs are reddish purple with orange dots (lenticels). Species name *discolor* refers to the pale underside of leaves. Look for tiny leaf-like stipules on the leafstalk and contrasting green upper and whitish lower leaf surfaces to help identify.

bark

fruit

Black Willow
Salix nigra

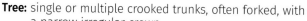

Family: Willow (Salicaceae)

Height: 40–60' (12–18 m)

Tree: single or multiple crooked trunks, often forked, with a narrow irregular crown

Leaf: simple, narrow lance-shaped, 3–6" (7.5–15 cm) in length, alternately attached, fine-toothed margin, shiny green above and below, short leafstalk often has tiny leaf-like appendages (stipules), making the leaf appear to be clasping the twig

Bark: dark brown color and deeply furrowed into large patchy scales with flat-topped ridges

Flower: catkin, 2–3" (5–7.5 cm) long, hanging down

Fruit: catkin-like fruit, 2–3" (5–7.5 cm) long, composed of many capsules, ¼" (.6 cm) long, seeds within

Fall Color: light yellow

Origin/Age: native; 50–75 years

Habitat: wet soils, stream banks, wetlands and other wet places, shade intolerant

Range: throughout

Stan's Notes: The largest native willow in the Carolinas. Common name comes from the dark bark. A fast-growing but short-lived tree that does not tolerate shade. Commonly found along streams, rivers and other wet places. Also called Swamp Willow. Frequently hybridizes with the Crack Willow (*S. fragilis*), a non-native European species. Twigs are light yellow to reddish and downy when young, becoming gray and hairless. Branches are spreading and easily broken by high winds. Look for its large leaves and leaf-like stipules to help identify.

bark

immature fruit

fruit

Sand Live Oak

Quercus geminata

Family: Beech (Fagaceae)

Height: 10–15' (3–4.5 m)

Tree: small to medium tree, single or multiple trunks, dense large broad crown, often forms thick stands of trees

Leaf: simple, oval, 1–4" (2.5–10 cm) long, alternately attached, thick and leathery, margin (edge) strongly rolled inward, evergreen, coarsely veined, dark green above, dull gray and densely hairy below

Bark: dark brown to reddish brown, thick, shallow furrows with flat scales and ridges

Fruit: green acorn, turning brown at maturity and grayish white hairy scales on cap, edible, ovate, ¾–1" (2–2.5 cm) long, cap covering upper third of nut, maturing in 1 season

Fall Color: green

Origin/Age: native; 150–250 years

Habitat: sandy soils, coastal dunes, often in pure stands, sun

Range: along the sandy coast of the Carolinas, sand dunes, often with pines

Stan's Notes: Small to medium tree often growing with others to form dense patch of evergreen trees. Called "Sand" because of where it likes to grow, in the sandy soils along the coast. Closely related to the Southern Live Oak. "Live" refers to the leaves, which remain green for most of the year. Native range along the coast from North Carolina, into southern Florida and to Mississippi. Commonly hybridizes with other Live Oak species.

bark

fruit

Willow Oak
Quercus phellos

SIMPLE
ALTERNATE

Family: Beech (Fagaceae)

Height: 50–80' (15–24.5 m)

Tree: medium to large tree, single straight trunk, thin branches with slender twigs, broad round crown

Leaf: simple, lance-shaped, 2–4" (5–10 cm) long and 1" (2.5 cm) wide, alternately attached, single tiny pointed tip (bristle-tipped), smooth (sometimes wavy) margin, light green, sometimes with tiny gray hairs on underside

Bark: dark gray, smooth and hard, becoming nearly black with narrow ridges with age

Fruit: green acorn, turning brown when mature, edible, nearly round, ½" (1 cm) long, on a short stalk, shallow cap covering upper third of nut, maturing in 2 seasons

Fall Color: yellow

Origin/Age: native; 150–200 years

Habitat: moist soils, floodplains, river valleys and other lowlands, sun to partial shade

Range: eastern half of the Carolinas, widely planted throughout along streets

Stan's Notes: This is a very different-looking oak, with thin willow-like leaves and twigs. A familiar tree, widely planted along streets as an ornamental tree and for shade. Tolerant of heat, drought and air pollution. Can survive with roots in standing water. Small acorns are eaten by all sorts of wildlife. Also called Peach Oak or Pin Oak (same common name, but not the Pin Oak on pg. 231).

bark

fruit

Live Oak
Quercus virginiana

Family: Beech (Fagaceae)

Height: 30–50' (9–15 m)

Tree: medium tree, extremely large single trunk, often divided at base into multiple large trunks, dense large broad crown up to 100' (30.5 m) wide

Leaf: simple, oval, 2–5" (5–12.5 cm) long, alternately attached, blunt tip with a single bristle, wavy margin with few (if any) teeth, thick, semi-evergreen to evergreen, dark green above, paler and a few hairs to densely hairy below

Bark: dark brown to reddish brown, thick, shallow furrows with flat scales and ridges

Fruit: green acorn, turning brown at maturity, edible, ovate, ¾–1" (2–2.5 cm) long, on a long stalk, cap covering upper half of nut, maturing in 1 season

Fall Color: green to brown

Origin/Age: native; 150–250 years

Habitat: sandy soils, coastal dunes, often in pure stands, sun

Range: along the coast of the Carolinas, planted throughout in parks and yards

Stan's Notes: Extremely large and handsome tree with large swooping lower branches that often touch the ground. Considered the ultimate shade tree due to its large spreading horizontal branches. Old trees are usually draped with Spanish moss, which gets its water and nutrients from the air and rain (epiphyte). Branches are also home to ferns and other epiphytic plants. "Live" refers to the leaves, which remain green for most of the year. Fast growing and long lived. Native range was just a thin strip along the coast, but now planted throughout the Carolinas. Has been successfully transplanted to the Southwest.

bark

fruit

Laurel Oak
Quercus laurifolia

Family: Beech (Fagaceae)

Height: 40–60' (12–18 m)

Tree: medium tree with a single straight trunk, dense broad round crown

Leaf: simple, lance- to diamond-shaped, 2–5" (5–12.5 cm) long, alternately attached, pointed tip, wavy tooth-less margin, semi-evergreen, shiny bright green above, paler below

Bark: dark brown to nearly black, thick, smooth when young, becoming deeply furrowed with broad flat ridges with age

Fruit: green acorn, turning brown to nearly black at maturity, bitter, nearly round, ½–¾" (1–2 cm) long, on short stalk, tiny scales on cap, shallow cap covering upper quarter of nut, maturing in 2 seasons

Fall Color: green to brown

Origin/Age: native; 75–100 years

Habitat: moist to wet soils, along rivers and other wet areas, sun to partial shade

Range: eastern half of the Carolinas, planted in parks and yards

Stan's Notes: A relatively fast-growing, short-lived tree known for its dense leaf growth that produces shade. Widely planted as a shade tree throughout the Carolinas. Lower branches tend to droop and need pruning to allow for pedestrian traffic. Semi-evergreen leaves are dropped in spring when growing new leaves. Common name "Laurel" and species name *laurifolia* refer to the leaves, which resemble those of Grecian laurel of the Mediterranean region.

bark

fruit

Shingle Oak
Quercus imbricaria

Family: Beech (Fagaceae)

Height: 50–60' (15–18 m)

Tree: medium tree, single straight trunk, wide spreading branches, wide round crown

Leaf: simple, oval to oblong (sometimes lance-shaped), 3–6" (7.5–15 cm) in length, alternately attached, pointed tip, edges wavy or slightly turned under, lacking teeth, shiny dark green above, light green with soft hairs below, midrib often yellowish

Bark: brown to gray, turning darker and more furrowed with age, thinner than the bark of most other oaks

Fruit: green acorn, turning brown when mature, edible, round, ½–¾" (1–2 cm) long, single or in pairs on a short stalk, cap covering the upper third to half of nut, maturing in 2 seasons

Fall Color: yellow to reddish brown

Origin/Age: native; 100–150 years

Habitat: moist soils, along streams and rivers, higher dry soils, sun

Range: scattered in isolated locations in North Carolina, planted in parks and yards

Stan's Notes: Often planted as an ornamental tree and for shade due to its large attractive foliage and tolerance of soil conditions. Moderate to fast growing, medium life span. Usually in moist sites with non-mature forests. Flowers in spring. Acorns mature in fall of the second year and are an important food for waterfowl such as Mallards and Wood Ducks. Wood is easy to split and was once used for roofing shingles, hence its common name. Wood is now sold as Red Oak. Holds its leaves into winter, making it a good windbreak.

bark

fruit

Chinquapin Oak
Quercus muehlenbergii

Family: Beech (Fagaceae)

Height: 50–70' (15–21 m)

Tree: medium tree, single straight trunk, narrow round crown composed mostly of many short thin twigs

Leaf: simple, 4–6" (10–15 cm) long, alternately attached, with pointed tip, many straight parallel veins, each ending in a curved coarse tooth, shiny dark green above, pale green and slightly hairy below

Bark: light gray to brown, many long narrow scales

Fruit: green acorn, turning brown when mature, ½–1" (1–2.5 cm) long, on a short stalk, cap covering the upper third of nut

Fall Color: red or brown

Origin/Age: native; 100–150 years

Habitat: sandy soils, dry rocky outcroppings, sun

Range: scattered locations in the western quarter of the Carolinas

Stan's Notes: Occurs in limestone rock outcroppings, ridges and other dry rocky sites. Common name comes from its leaves, which resemble those of trees in a group known as chinquapin. Also called Yellow Oak or Chestnut Oak, the latter name referring to the shape of the leaves, which resemble American Chestnut (pg. 199). Species name given in honor of botanist Gotthilf Henry Ernst Muhlenberg (1753–1815). While most other oaks have lobed leaves, this oak has simple leaves of variable size that tend to be gathered at the tips of branches. A member of the white oak group, producing mature acorns in one season unlike red oaks, which take two seasons to produce mature acorns.

bark

fruit

Swamp Chestnut Oak
Quercus michauxii

Family: Beech (Fagaceae)

Height: 50–80' (15–24.5 m)

Tree: medium to large tree, single straight trunk, narrow round crown

Leaf: simple, oval, 4–9" (10–22.5 cm) long, alternately attached, wavy margin with many coarse rounded teeth, shiny green above, paler with gray-to-green hairs below

Bark: light gray, thick with irregular furrows and scales

Fruit: green acorn, turning brown when mature, edible, egg-shaped (ovate), 1–1½" (2.5–4 cm) long, on a short stalk, thick cap covering the upper third of nut, maturing in 1 season

Fall Color: red to brown

Origin/Age: native; 150–200 years

Habitat: moist soils, floodplains, river valleys, sun to partial shade

Range: eastern half of the Carolinas

Stan's Notes: Known for its large, fuzzy, coarsely toothed leaves and large acorns. Common name "Chestnut" refers to its leaves, which appear similar to the toothed leaves of American Chestnut (pg. 199). Sometimes called Cow Oak, presumably because cows eat the acorns. Acorns are also eaten by wildlife such as turkeys, deer and squirrels. Unlike other acorns, these are less bitter and can be eaten without boiling out the tannin. Lumber is hard and strong and has been used in flooring, furniture and tool handles. Baskets have been woven from its wood fibers. Also known as Basket Oak. Given the species name *michauxii* for French botanist and explorer André Michaux, who collected plants in the U.S. during the last half of the eighteenth century.

bark

fruit

Chestnut Oak
Quercus montana

Family: Beech (Fagaceae)

Height: 60–90' (18–27.5 m)

Tree: large tree with a straight trunk, broad open crown, often irregular

Leaf: simple, 4–8" (10–20 cm) in length, 2–4" (5–10 cm) wide, alternately attached, elliptical, rounded or pointed tip, tapering at the base, widest beyond the middle, irregular coarse-toothed margin, shiny yellow-green and almost leathery above, paler and finely hairy below

Bark: light to dark brown with deep narrow furrows

Fruit: green acorn, turning brown when mature, edible, egg-shaped (ovate), ¾–1¼" (2–3 cm) long, on a short stalk, thin cap covering upper third of nut

Fall Color: yellow to dull orange

Origin/Age: native; 200–500 years

Habitat: sandy, gravelly upland sites, hillsides, well-drained lowland sites, sun

Range: western half of the Carolinas

Stan's Notes: This slow-growing tree, also known as Rock Oak, is suited for planting on dry rocky soils as a shade tree. Grows on hills and mountainsides up to 4,000 feet (1,220 m). Large toothed leaves resemble chestnut tree leaves, hence its common name. Male and female flowers bloom on the same tree. Produces edible acorns each year, but has a large crop every 4–7 years. Acorns are an important food crop to wildlife such as turkeys and deer. Bark contains more tannin than most other oaks. The tannin was extracted and used in tanning leather. Its strong, heavy, light brown wood is often sold as White Oak. Native to the eastern U.S. north of central Mississippi.

thorn

bark

flower

fruit

American Plum
Prunus americana

Family: Rose (Rosaceae)

Height: 10–15' (3–4.5 m)

Tree: small tree, single trunk, rarely over 6" (15 cm) in diameter, many branches

Leaf: simple, oblong to oval, 2–5" (5–12.5 cm) in length, alternately attached, pointed tip, double-toothed margin, network of veins, dark green

Bark: reddish brown or gray to white in color with large light-colored horizontal marks (lenticels), smooth, breaking into large scales or plates, large sharp thorns, 1–3" (2.5–7.5 cm) long

Flower: showy white flower, 1" (2.5 cm) wide, in clusters, 3–5" (7.5–12.5 cm) wide, very fragrant

Fruit: large fleshy red plum (drupe), edible, 1" (2.5 cm) wide, containing 1 large seed

Fall Color: golden yellow

Origin/Age: native; 25–30 years

Habitat: moist soils, in open fields, along woodland edges, shade intolerant

Range: western half of the Carolinas

Stan's Notes: A fast-growing ornamental tree also known as Wild Plum. Shade intolerant, preferring open sunny sites. Flowers are large and attractive. Resulting plums are highly prized by wildlife and people. Plums make good jellies and jams; can be eaten fresh. Twigs often smell of bitter almond when they are crushed. The large sharp thorns (see inset) are actually modified branches. In pioneer times, its thorns were used for mending clothes and other tasks.

bark

flower

fruit

Pin Cherry
Prunus pensylvanica

SIMPLE
ALTERNATE

Family: Rose (Rosaceae)

Height: 10–30' (3–9 m)

Tree: single straight or crooked trunk, narrow crown

Leaf: simple, lance-shaped, 2–5" (5–12.5 cm) in length, alternately attached, frequently curved backward, tapering to a point, fine-toothed and often wavy margin, shiny green above and below, 2 small swellings (glands) on the leafstalk near leaf base, leaves often clustered at ends of branches

Bark: gray to nearly black in color, smooth and shiny when young, brown-to-orange marks (lenticels) with age, sometimes peeling into papery strips, pleasant scent when scraped

Flower: 5-petaled white flower, ½" (1 cm) wide, on a long stalk, in clusters, 1–2" (2.5–5 cm) long

Fruit: green cherry (drupe), turning bright red when mature, edible, ¼" (.6 cm) diameter, on a very long red fruit stalk

Fall Color: purplish red

Origin/Age: native; 20–40 years

Habitat: dry soils, open hillsides, fields, sun

Range: western quarter of the Carolinas

Stan's Notes: Also called Wild Red Cherry, Bird Cherry or Fire Cherry. Common name "Fire" refers to its habit of growing quickly after fires. An important pioneer species, invading openings created by logging, fire or abandoned fields. A great food source for wildlife. Its cherries are especially good in jellies and were once used in cough medicines. Long stalks of the flowers and fruit help differentiate it from Black Cherry (pg. 137).

midrib hairs

immature fruit

bark

flower

fruit

Black Cherry
Prunus serotina

Family: Rose (Rosaceae)

Height: 50–75' (15–23 m)

Tree: uniformly thick trunk shows little tapering, often tilted or bent, with few lower branches and open round crown

Leaf: simple, lance-shaped, 2–6" (5–15 cm) long, alternately attached, with a unique inward-curved tip resembling a bird's beak, fine-toothed margin, row of fine brown hairs along midrib underneath (see inset), shiny dark green above, paler below

Bark: dark reddish brown to black in color with large, conspicuous curving scales (like potato chips), green inner bark tastes bitter, but smells pleasant

Flower: white flower, ½" (1 cm) wide, 6–12 per elongated cluster, 4–6" (10–15 cm) long

Fruit: green cherry (drupe), red to dark blue or black at maturity, edible, ¼–½" (.6–1 cm) wide, in clusters

Fall Color: yellow

Origin/Age: native; 125–150 years

Habitat: wide variety soils, mixed with deciduous species

Range: throughout

Stan's Notes: Largest of the cherry trees. Widely sought for its wonderfully rich brown wood. Several species of *Prunus* in the Carolinas, this one producing a tart but edible fruit. An important food crop for birds and wildlife. Black knot (a fungus) is the most common disease of Black Cherry, resulting in large black growths along twigs and small branches, leading to die-back of affected branches.

bark

fruit

Black Tupelo
Nyssa sylvatica

SIMPLE ALTERNATE

Family: Dogwood (Nyssaceae)

Height: 50–70' (15–21 m)

Tree: narrow conical tree, single trunk, many slender, often horizontal branches, round crown

Leaf: simple, oval, 2–5" (5–12.5 cm) long, alternately attached, usually widest above center of leaf, wavy toothless margin, shiny green above, paler and often hairy below, leafstalk often red, leaves often clustered at ends of branches

Bark: light gray to light brown, flaky texture with thick irregular rectangular ridges

Fruit: green berry-like fruit (drupe), turning blue-black when mature, ½" (1 cm) wide, containing 1 seed

Fall Color: red

Origin/Age: native; 50–100 years

Habitat: moist to wet soils, along streams or wetlands, part shade

Range: throughout

Stan's Notes: A common species throughout the eastern U.S. from New England to Florida. This is a medium-sized tree, often planted as an ornamental for its red leaves in fall and its autumn-ripening fruit, which birds and mammals eat. In southern states, bees that collect nectar from its spring flowers produce Tupelo honey. Also called Black-gum, Sour-gum or Pepperidge. Reproduces by sprouts growing from its roots. The genus name is derived from the Greek word Nysa, the mythical region in Greece where water nymphs werepresumed to live; it originally described another *Nyssa* species that grows in swamps, the Water Tupelo (pg. 143). Species name *sylvatica* means "of the woods," describing its habitat.

bark

fruit

Swamp Tupelo
Nyssa biflora

Family: Dogwood (Nyssaceae)

Height: 50–80' (15–24 m)

Tree: tall narrow tree with swollen trunk base, usually a single trunk, dense crown with slender branches, round crown

Leaf: simple, oval, 2–5" (5–13 cm) long, alternately attached, usually widest above center of leaf, wavy toothless margin, shiny green above, paler and often hairy below

Bark: light gray to light brown, flaky texture with thick irregular rectangular flat ridges

Fruit: green berry-like fruit (drupe), turning blue-black when mature, ½" (1 cm) wide, containing 1 seed

Fall Color: red, gold and orange

Origin/Age: native; 50–100 years

Habitat: swampy edges, moist to wet soils, along streams or wetlands, part shade, up to 4,000' (1,220 m) elevation

Range: common throughout both states

Stan's Notes: Very similar to Black Tupelo (pg. 139) but has an enlarged or swollen trunk base. Some reproduction is from seeds, which are often eaten by birds and deposited later in droppings. Germinates when water recedes, but the sprout will die if covered with water, so it must grow fast to keep ahead of rising water. Also reproduces by sprouts growing from its roots. Tolerates flooding, which kills most other trees, but doesn't live in deeper-water areas that never dry out. Flowers appear in spring (April) and are pollinated by insects, primarily bees. The base is swollen to the average height of the water level during the growing season. Species name *biflora* means "two flowers," describing its flower cluster.

bark

immature fruit

fruit

Water Tupelo
Nyssa aquatica

Family: Dogwood (Nyssaceae)

Height: 80–100' (24.5–30.5 m)

Tree: large tree, single straight trunk with a flared base (buttress), few low branches, many short branches clustering near crown

Leaf: simple, obovate, 5–8" (12.5–20 cm) long, alternately attached, few irregular teeth, thick, shiny green above, paler below and sometimes with hairs near midrib, long hairy leafstalk

Bark: dark brown to reddish brown, smooth, becoming furrowed with scaly ridges with age

Fruit: green berry-like fruit (drupe), turning dark purple at maturity, thin sour pulp, oblong, 1" (2.5 cm) long, containing 1 seed

Fall Color: yellow

Origin/Age: native; 100–150 years

Habitat: wet soils, swamps, floodplains, in standing water, partial shade to sun

Range: eastern half of the Carolinas

Stan's Notes: This is an aquatic tree, hence its common name. Not uncommon for it to grow where standing water covers its roots for several months. The buttress helps to stabilize and hold the tree upright in water-saturated soil. The genus *Nyssa* is a Greek word that refers to the home of the water nymphs. Also called Swamp Tupelo, Cotton-gum, Water-gum or Sour-gum, the latter being another common name for Black Tupelo (pg. 139). The tall straight trunk yields good lumber for furniture and other building projects. Fruit matures in early fall and is eaten by wildlife such as bear, raccoons, Wood Ducks, turkeys and other birds.

bark

flower

fruit

Sweetbay
Magnolia virginiana

Family: Magnolia (Magnoliaceae)

Height: 20–40' (6–12 m)

Tree: small to medium tree, many thin trunks from a central base, narrow pointed crown

Leaf: simple, oblong, 3–6" (7.5–15 cm) long, alternately attached, smooth margin, slightly thick, semi-evergreen, shiny green above, paler with white to silver hairs below, short leafstalk

Bark: gray, smooth

Flower: cup-shaped creamy white flower, 2–3" (5–7.5 cm) wide, made of 9–12 petals, solitary at the end of branch, lemony fragrance

Fruit: smooth green aggregate, turning red at maturity, cone-shaped, 1–2" (2.5–5 cm) long, splitting open in autumn and releasing many bright red seeds

Fall Color: green to yellow

Origin/Age: native; 50–100 years

Habitat: wet soils, along coastal wetlands, rivers and streams, sun to partial shade

Range: eastern half of the Carolinas, planted in parks and yards

Stan's Notes: A much-loved magnolia with fragrant leaves and intensely lemon-scented flowers. Flowers start to bloom in mid-June and continue blooming into the summer. Cone-shaped fruit is smooth, unlike the fuzzy fruit of other magnolias. Fruit opens in fall to release red seeds. "Bay" in the common name comes from early botanists, who referred to all evergreen trees with broad leaves as bays. Also called Sweetbay Magnolia or Swamp Magnolia.

bark

flower

fruit

Cucumbertree
Magnolia acuminata

Family: Magnolia (Magnoliaceae)

Height: 40–60' (12–18 m)

Tree: medium-sized tree, straight trunk, short, upright spreading branches, narrow pointed crown

Leaf: simple, oval, 5–10" (12.5–25 cm) long (sometimes larger), alternately attached, pointed tip, round at the base, wavy or smooth toothless margin, green above, paler below with soft fine hairs

Bark: brown with narrow furrowed rows

Flower: large 6-petaled white-to-yellow flower, 2–3½" (5–9 cm) wide, solitary at the end of branch in spring

Fruit: green aggregate, turning dark red when mature, cone-shaped, 1½–2½" (4–6 cm) long, on a long fruit stalk at the end of branch

Fall Color: dull yellow or brown

Origin/Age: native; 125–150 years

Habitat: wide variety of soils from moist to dry, usually in moist valleys, partial shade

Range: western half of the Carolinas

Stan's Notes: This species is the largest and hardiest of our native magnolias. Originally widespread and abundant. Now also planted widely as an ornamental because it is fast growing and long lived. Takes 25–30 years to reach flowering size. Produces flowers and fruit each year with large seed crops every 3–5 years. Seeds are eaten by many bird and mammal species. Often grows large enough to be harvested for lumber. Common name comes from its unripened fruit, which looks like a cucumber.

bark

flower

fruit

Southern Magnolia
Magnolia grandiflora

Family: Magnolia (Magnoliaceae)

Height: 60–80' (18–24.5 m)

Tree: medium to large tree, single straight trunk, large conical crown

Leaf: simple, elliptical, 5–10" (12.5–25 cm) long, alternately attached, toothless margin, thick, leathery, evergreen, shiny green above, paler with rusty hairs below

Bark: medium to dark gray, smooth when young, large scaly patches with age

Flower: large cup-shaped white flower, 6–10" (15–25 cm) wide, solitary at the end of branch, very fragrant

Fruit: large green aggregate, turning red at maturity, cone-shaped, 3–6" (7.5–15 cm) long, covered with woolly hairs, splitting open in autumn and releasing seeds that hang on slender silken threads

Fall Color: green

Origin/Age: native; 50–100 years

Habitat: moist soils, deciduous forests, sun to part shade

Range: coastal plains in South Carolina, scattered in south-eastern North Carolina, planted throughout both states in parks and yards

Stan's Notes: A favorite tree to plant as an ornamental because of its large fragrant flowers or for shade. Several cultivated varieties now exist, with hardy varieties planted as far north as New York. Flowers from April through June. Fruit matures in September and October, releasing many seeds when fruit opens. Each seed hangs temporarily from a slender silken thread before falling to the ground. Also called Evergreen Magnolia, Bullbay or Large-flower Magnolia.

bark

fruit

Ginkgo
Ginkgo biloba

Family: Ginkgo (Ginkgoaceae)

Height: 40–60' (12–18 m)

Tree: pyramid shape, single straight trunk and narrow tapering crown

Leaf: simple, fan-shaped, 1–3" (2.5–7.5 cm) wide, alternately attached, 1 or more notches along margin, shallow irregular teeth, no midrib, veins straight and parallel (sometimes forked)

Bark: gray, irregularly rough with many furrows

Fruit: foul-smelling yellow fruit with thick, fleshy outer coat when ripe, 1" (2.5 cm) in diameter, on a long thin fruit stalk

Fall Color: yellow

Origin/Age: non-native, introduced from eastern China; 100–150 years

Habitat: well-drained soils, sun to partial shade

Range: planted in yards and parks and along roads, not found growing in the wild

Stan's Notes: Gingko trees have been cultivated in China, Japan, and Korea for about a thousand years. But wild trees were thoughtto be extinct until native populations were discovered in China. Only the male trees are sold and planted since female trees produce butyric acid, which makes the fruit smell foul. Ginkgo fruit has been highly prized by some people for medicinal properties. Its leaves are often in two lobes, hence the species name *biloba*. Also called Maidenhair-tree because the unique fan-shaped leaves resemble the fronds of the Maidenhair Fern plant.

flower

bark

fruit

thorn

Russian-olive

Elaeagnus angustifolia

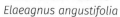

Family: Oleaster (Elaeagnaceae)

Height: 10–20' (3–6 m)

Tree: single crooked trunk is often divided low, open irregular crown

Leaf: simple, lance-shaped, 1–4" (2.5–10 cm) in length, alternately attached, blunt tip or sharp tip, margin lacking teeth, gray above and below, leaves and twigs covered with grayish white hairs

Bark: light gray with shallow furrows, thorns on twigs

Flower: 4-petaled yellow flower, ¼–½" (.6–1 cm) wide

Fruit: dry gray-to-yellow olive-like fruit (drupe), ¼–½" (.6–1 cm) diameter, containing 1 seed

Fall Color: brown

Origin/Age: non-native, introduced from Europe; 50–75 years

Habitat: wide variety of soils, sun to partial shade

Range: usually seen near old farmsteads, parks, formerly planted as an ornamental

Stan's Notes: Was planted in North America for its unusual gray leaves and olive-like fruit, often as a shelterbelt. While it's no longer planted, it has escaped from gardens, yards and parks and now grows in the wild (naturalized). Spread by birds, which pass the seeds through their digestive tracts unharmed. Twigs are often scaly and armed with very long thorns (see inset) that have a salmon-colored pith. The species name *angustifolia* means "narrow leaf." Also called Oleaster or Narrow-leaved Oleaster.

bark

flower

fruit

Wax-myrtle
Myrica cerifera

SIMPLE
ALTERNATE

Family: Bayberry (Myricaceae)

Height: 15–30' (4.5–9 m)

Tree: small tree, often appearing like a large shrub, multiple small trunks, broad round crown

Leaf: simple, lance-shaped, 1–5" (2.5–12.5 cm) long, alternately attached, coarse-toothed margin beyond the middle, thick, aromatic, evergreen, shiny yellowish green or grayish green above, paler with yellow dots below

Bark: light gray, thin and smooth

Flower: small red flower, ½" (1 cm) long, in compact oval clusters, located at leaf base

Fruit: warty green berry (drupe), covered with bluish wax when mature, round, ⅛" (.3 cm) wide, in clusters, containing 1 seed

Fall Color: green

Origin/Age: native; 50–100 years

Habitat: sandy soils, swamps, pinelands, sun to part shade

Range: eastern half of the Carolinas

Stan's Notes: Clusters of bluish berries make this an attractive ornamental to plant in yards, and they also attract much wildlife. Planted around homes for the aromatic oils in the leaves, which are reported to repel insects. Can be pruned to appear like a shrub. A hardy tree that can tolerate a wide range of growing conditions, such as high salt concentrations in the soil. Usually an evergreen, but will drop its leaves in winter if it gets too cold. A sprig of leaves placed in a drawer or closet is supposed to keep insect pests away. Many settlers used the wax from the berries to make candles.

thorn

bark

flower

fruit

Hawthorn

Crataegus spp.

Family: Rose (Rosaceae)

Height: 15–25' (4.5–7.5 m)

Tree: short round tree, single trunk, flat-topped crown

Leaf: simple, oval to triangular, 2–4" (5–10 cm) in length, alternately attached, sometimes 3 lobes, double-toothed margin, thick and shiny, dark green above and below

Bark: gray with red patches, very scaly and covered with peeling bark, sturdy thorns, 1–3" (2.5–7.5 cm) in length, on branches

Flower: 5-petaled white (occasionally pink) flower, 1–2" (2.5–5 cm) diameter, in flat-topped clusters, 3–5" (7.5–12.5 cm) wide, fragrant

Fruit: red (sometimes orange) apple-like fruit (pome), edible, ½–1" (1–2.5 cm) diameter, in clusters

Fall Color: red to orange

Origin/Age: native and non-native; 50–100 years

Habitat: dry soils, open fields, hillsides, sun

Range: scattered in isolated locations throughout the Carolinas, planted in yards and parks

Stan's Notes: One of over 100 species in North America. Because of its affinity to hybridize, there are more than 1,100 different kinds of hawthorn in the U.S., making it difficult to distinguish each. Fruit is edible and eaten by many bird and animal species. Branches and trunk are armed with long sturdy thorns that allow shrikes, also known as Butcher Birds, to impale their prey on the spines. Birds like to build their nests in this tree, gaining some protection from the large sharp thorns. Also called Thornapple or Haws.

bark

flower

fruit

Juneberry
Amelanchier arborea

Family: Rose (Rosaceae)

Height: 10–20' (3–6 m)

Tree: multiple narrow trunks, round crown

Leaf: simple, oval, 2–4" (5–10 cm) in length, alternately attached, pointed tip, fine-toothed margin (sometimes toothless near stalk), dark green above, whitish hairs below and covering stalk

Bark: light gray, smooth with shallow cracks

Flower: erect white flower, 1" (2.5 cm) long, in clusters, 1–3" (2.5–7.5 cm) wide

Fruit: red berry-like fruit (pome), turning dark blue at maturity, edible, round, ¼" (.6 cm) diameter, on a fruit stalk, in hanging clusters

Fall Color: yellow to red

Origin/Age: native; 10–20 years

Habitat: dry soils, hillsides, forest edges, open fields, sun

Range: western half of the Carolinas

Stan's Notes: There are up to 20 species of *Amelanchier* in the world, most occurring in North America. Several varieties of Juneberry, but they are hard to differentiate because of crossbreeding among species. Called Juneberry because the fruit ripens in June. Fruit is edible and an important source of food for wildlife. Also known as Downy Serviceberry, "Downy" for the whitish downy hairs on the underside of leaves and covering the leafstalks, and "Serviceberry" because it flowers in spring coincidentally when cemetery burials were historically held in northern climates. Also known as Shadbush because the blooming time occurs when shad (a kind of fish) spawn.

bark

fruit

American Holly
Ilex opaca

Family: Holly (Aquifoliaceae)

Height: 40–60' (12–18 m)

Tree: medium tree with a single straight trunk and long, narrow tapering crown

Leaf: simple, elliptical, 2–4" (5–10 cm) long, alternately attached, coarse-toothed margin with spiny tips, thick and leathery evergreen leaves, green above, yellow-green below

Bark: light gray, thin and smooth, sometimes with warty growths

Fruit: green berry-like fruit (drupe), ¼–⅓" (.6–.8 cm) wide, turning bright red when mature, on a short fruit stalk, containing 4 tiny nutlets

Fall Color: green

Origin/Age: native; 50–100 years

Habitat: moist to moderately wet soils, floodplains, mixed deciduous forests, shade tolerant

Range: throughout

Stan's Notes: There are more than 600 species of *Ilex* worldwide, with about a dozen native to the eastern and southern U.S. Of these, six species grow large enough to be considered trees. Ripe fruit is red and only rarely orange, maturing in late summer and fall and remaining on the tree well into winter. Fruit is bitter, but eaten by a wide variety of birds and some mammals. Seen growing along hedgerows, where birds have deposited seeds unharmed. Cut branches with evergreen leaves and bright red fruit are popular for holiday decorating.

mature fruit

bark

flower

fruit

Ironwood
Ostrya virginiana

Family: Birch (Betulaceae)

Height: 20–40' (6–12 m)

Tree: single trunk that is often crooked, with spreading branches, open irregular crown

Leaf: simple, oval, 2–4" (5–10 cm) in length, alternately attached, with pointed tip, asymmetrical leaf base, double-toothed margin, fuzzy to touch, yellowish green color

Bark: gray, fibrous with narrow ridges spiraling around the trunk

Flower: catkin, ½–1" (1–2.5 cm) long

Fruit: flattened nutlet, ¼" (.6 cm) wide, within a hanging cluster of inflated sacs that are green when young, turning brown at maturity, 1½–2" (4–5 cm) long, appearing like the fruit of the hop plant

Fall Color: yellow

Origin/Age: native; 75–100 years

Habitat: dry soils, slopes, ridges, shade tolerant

Range: western half of the Carolinas

Stan's Notes: An important understory tree, frequently spending its entire life in the shade of other taller trees. The common name refers to its very strong and heavy wood, which is used to make tool handles and tent stakes. Distinctive thin scaly bark that spirals up the trunk and velvety soft leaves make this tree easy to identify. Also called Hop-hornbeam in direct reference to the fruit sacs, which appear like hops. One of three species of *Ostrya* in North America.

bark

flower

Mountain-laurel
Kalmia latifolia

Family: Heath (Ericaceae)

Height: 10–20' (3–6 m)

Tree: small tree, multiple thin crooked trunks, stout spreading branches, irregular crown

Leaf: simple, lance-shaped, 2½–4" (6–10 cm) in length, alternately attached, may be oppositely attached or in whorls of 3 leaves, hard white tip, wavy toothless margin, thick and stiff, semi-evergreen, dull dark green above, yellow-green below

Bark: dark reddish brown with long narrow ridges

Flower: 5-lobed saucer-shaped pink or white flower with purple lines, ½–1" (1–2.5 cm) diameter, in round clusters, 4–5" (10–12.5 cm) diameter, at the end of a long stalk covered with sticky hairs

Fruit: dark brown capsule, rounded with a long thread-like structure at tip, ¼" (.6 cm) wide, covered with sticky hairs, splitting open along 5 lines, containing many fine seeds

Fall Color: green to brown

Origin/Age: native; 25–30 years

Habitat: moist acid soils, understory of mature mountain forests and mixed forests on slopes, shade

Range: western two-thirds of the Carolinas, widely planted in parks and yards

Stan's Notes: Often in large dense stands in which birds and animals nest or hide. Planted for its foliage and beautiful springtime flowers. Leaves are toxic to people, but are eaten by wildlife, such as White-tailed Deer. Color and scent of flowers attracts bees. Seeds are released in late fall. Fruit remains on tree until the next summer.

bark

Blue Beech
Carpinus caroliniana

Family: Birch (Betulaceae)

Height: 15–25' (4.5–7.5 m)

Tree: single to multiple crooked trunks, wide and often flat crown

Leaf: simple, oval, 2–5" (5–12.5 cm) length, alternately attached, with pointed tip, asymmetrical leaf base, margin is fine, sharp and double-toothed, color is light green

Bark: light blue-gray to gray, very smooth and unbroken with longitudinal muscle-like ridges

Fruit: many small ribbed nutlets, each ¼" (.6 cm) wide, contained in a leaf-like papery green bract, 2–4" (5–10 cm) long, that hangs in clusters and turns brown when mature

Fall Color: orange to deep red

Origin/Age: native; 50–75 years

Habitat: rich moist soils, moist valleys, along streams and other wet places, partial shade

Range: throughout

Stan's Notes: One of about 25 species of *Carpinus*, Blue Beech is the only native of North America. An easily recognized understory tree, with its smooth unbroken trunk and long, fluted muscle-like ridges. Also known as Musclewood, Water Beech, Ironwood (same common name, but not the Ironwood on pg. 163) or the American Hornbeam. In the latter name, "Horn" means "tough" and "beam" means "tree" in Old English, which describes its tough wood. The wood is used for tool handles.

bark

fruit

American Beech
Fagus grandifolia

Family: Beech (Fagaceae)

Height: 60–80' (18–24.5 m)

Tree: medium to large tree, a short, thick single trunk branching close to ground, branches often droop to the ground, broad spreading round crown

Leaf: simple, oval, 2–5" (5–12.5 cm) in length, alternately attached, long pointed tip, straight parallel veins, each ends in a sharp shallow tooth, leathery dark green above, lighter green below

Bark: light gray, smooth

Fruit: reddish brown capsule, ½–1½" (1–4 cm) in length, in pairs, splitting open into 4 sections to release a 3-sided nut

Fall Color: yellow to brown

Origin/Age: native; 150–200 years

Habitat: well-drained moist soils and bottomlands, shade tolerant

Range: throughout

Stan's Notes: Highly prized tree with important benefits to wildlife. Squirrels, grouse, bear, raccoons, deer and many other animals eat the abundant and edible beechnuts. Unusual bark in that it remains smooth even as the tree matures. The wood is very valuable and has been used for many years in furniture and flooring. One of the most abundant, well-recognized trees in eastern North America. Grows in mixed deciduous forests with oaks and maples. Can grow in pure stands. This tree has been planted in parks and around homes for many years. Until a larger tree falls, allowing enough light and room to grow, young saplings can sustain in dense shade for years.

bark

flower

fruit

Alternate-leaf Dogwood
Cornus alternifolia

Family: Dogwood (Cornaceae)

Height: 25–35' (7.5–11 m)

Tree: small understory tree, usually a single trunk with multi-horizontal tiers of branches, resulting in a layered appearance

Leaf: simple, oval, 2–5" (5–12.5 cm) in length, alternately attached, pointed tip, margin lacking teeth, deep-curving (arcuate) parallel veins, dark green above, whitish below, leaves are often clustered at ends of the branches

Bark: gray, thin and smooth

Flower: a small white-to-cream flower, ¼–½" (.6–1 cm) wide, in round clusters, 3–5" (7.5–12.5 cm) wide

Fruit: green berry-like fruit (drupe), turning white to blue to nearly black at maturity, round, ¼" (.6 cm) diameter, on a red fruit stalk

Fall Color: red

Origin/Age: native; 40–60 years

Habitat: well-drained open woodlands, forest edges, shade

Range: western quarter of the Carolinas

Stan's Notes: A common understory tree that rarely gets taller than 35 feet (11 m), typically cultivated as an ornamental tree for landscaping. Its alternately attached leaves are unique, as other dogwoods have oppositely attached leaves. Branches are distinctly horizontal, growing in tiers, hence another common name, Pagoda Dogwood. "Pagoda" refers to a type of religious building in the East Asia that has many stories or levels, just like the many levels of branches on this tree. Look for the clusters of oval leaves near ends of branches.

fruit

bark

Red Mulberry
Morus rubra

Family: Mulberry (Moraceae)

Height: 20–30' (6–9 m)

Tree: single trunk, divided low, with spreading branches and dense round crown

Leaf: simple, oval to multi-lobed, 2–5" (5–12.5 cm) in length, alternately attached, with coarse-toothed margin, exudes milky sap when torn, shiny green above, hairy tufts below

Bark: gray to reddish brown with uneven furrows

Fruit: green berry (aggregate fruit), turning red to black, appearing like a raspberry, made up of many tiny 1-seeded fruit, sweet and edible, ½" (1 cm) wide

Fall Color: yellow

Origin/Age: native; 50–75 years

Habitat: moist soils, floodplains, river valleys, sun to partial shade

Range: throughout, formerly planted in parks and yards

Stan's Notes: This species produces large crops of fruit, providing an important food source for wildlife, especially birds. In summer, berries ripen to red and are delicious when black. Fruit is sweet and juicy and used in jams, jellies and pies. New trees are started when seeds pass through the digestive tracts of birds unharmed and are deposited. Its common name and the species name *rubra* refer to its mostly red fruit. Early settlers and American Indians used its fresh fruit to make beverages, cakes and preserves, and medicinally to treat dysentery and other ailments. Formerly planted in parks and yards, but fell out of favor due to the overabundance of fruit.

bark

flower

fruit

Eastern Redbud
Cercis canadensis

Family: Pea or Bean (Fabaceae)

Height: 15–25' (4.5–7.5 m)

Tree: small tree, single or multiple thin trunks with low branching, horizontal branching on umbrella-like spreading crown

Leaf: simple, heart-shaped, 2–6" (5–15 cm) in length, alternately attached, pointed tip, smooth margin, shiny dark green, leafstalk swollen at the top

Bark: gray, smooth with reddish streaks, becoming scaly with age

Flower: pea-like lavender-to-pink flower, ¼" (.6 cm) wide, along the branches

Fruit: reddish brown pod, 2–4" (5–10 cm) long, pointed at both ends, on a short stalk

Fall Color: yellow

Origin/Age: native; 50–75 years

Habitat: moist soils, along streams, forest edges, shade

Range: throughout, planted in parks and gardens

Stan's Notes: Also known as American Redbud or Judas-tree, the latter name referring to a legend that Judas hung himself from a redbud tree, and that the once-white flowers are now forever red with shame. An understory tree that tolerates shade, it would not be spring in many places without its spectacular display of pink flowers, which appear before the leaves. One of two *Cercis* species native to North America. The second species is found in California, Arizona and Nevada.

bark

flower

fruit

Carolina Silverbell
Halesia carolina

Family: Storax (Styracaceae)

Height: 20–40' (6–12 m)

Tree: small to medium tree, single straight trunk, narrow open crown

Leaf: simple, oval, 2–6" (5–15 cm) long, alternately attached, fine-toothed margin, dark green above, paler with short white hairs on veins below

Bark: brown to reddish-brown, furrowed with many long, narrow scaly ridges

Flower: 4-petaled bell-shaped white flower, ½–1" (1–2.5 cm) long, on a long stalk, 2–5 per hanging cluster

Fruit: 4-winged pod-like green fruit (drupe), turning brown and papery at maturity, 1–2" (2.5–5 cm) long, in hanging clusters, containing 2–3 seeds

Fall Color: yellow

Origin/Age: native; 50–100 years

Habitat: moist to wet soils, along streams, wetlands, partial shade to sun

Range: western half of the Carolinas, planted in parks and yards

Stan's Notes: Also called Mountain Silverbell since it often grows in mountainous regions. Frequently planted and pruned to keep as a spreading shrub or small tree. Attractive white flowers make it desirable to plant in gardens. In spring, the flowers attract many bees, which produce flavorful honey. Squirrels and other small mammals eat the fruit in fall. Once established, not much watering is needed, and the tree is pest- and disease-free. Although the tree doesn't grow very large, its wood has been used for cabinetry and carving. Also called Snowdrop-tree or Opossum-wood.

bark

flower

fruit

Redbay
Persea borbonia

SIMPLE ALTERNATE

Family: Laurel (Lauraceae)

Height: 40–60' (12–18 m)

Tree: medium-sized tree, short trunk divided into multiple small trunks, dense round crown

Leaf: simple, lance-shaped, 2–6" (5–15 cm) long, alternately attached, thick, aromatic, evergreen, bright green above, paler with white hairs below

Bark: dark red to brown, thin when young, becoming furrowed with age

Flower: light yellow flower, ⅓" (.8 cm) wide, on a short stalk, ½–1" (1–2.5 cm) long, in small clusters

Fruit: green berry (drupe), turning shiny black when mature, round, ½" (1 cm) wide, on a fruit stalk, ½–1" (1–2.5 cm) long, containing many seeds

Fall Color: green

Origin/Age: native; 50–100 years

Habitat: moist to wet soils, along streams and swamps, partial shade to full sun

Range: eastern half of the Carolinas, planted in parks and yards

Stan's Notes: A member of the Laurel family and closely related to Sassafras (pg. 221). Its aromatic leaves are used to flavor soups and meats. The leaves have been used as a substitute for bay leaves, a common herb that usually comes from the Bay Laurel, a European species in the same family. Squirrels and birds eat the bitter fruit. Wood has been used in boat construction and furniture. Planted along streets and parking lots and in other urban areas because of its ability to tolerate a variety of growing conditions.

immature fruit

bark

flower

fruit

Common Persimmon
Diospyros virginiana

Family: Ebony (Ebenaceae)

Height: 30–40' (9–12 m)

Tree: small to medium tree, single straight trunk, many short branches, dense cylindrical crown

Leaf: simple, oval to elliptical, 2–6" (5–15 cm) in length, alternately attached, with pointed tip, round base, smooth margin, no teeth, shiny dark green above, whitish green below

Bark: brown to nearly black, thick and deeply furrowed into small squares

Flower: tiny white-to-cream bell-shaped, 4-lobed flower ½–¾" (1–2 cm) long, solitary at base of leafstalk

Fruit: fleshy, smooth-skinned orange-to-purplish-brown berry, wrinkled when mature, round, ¾–1½" (2–4 cm) wide, short stalk, many flat brown seeds

Fall Color: yellow

Origin/Age: native; 100–200 years

Habitat: wide variety of soils, river valleys, dry upland sites

Range: throughout

Stan's Notes: Popular native tree, often planted for its glossy leaves and attractive square-patterned bark. Not easily transplanted due to its large taproot. Known for its large edible fruit, which ripens in fall and is a source of food for mammals and birds. Ripe fruit tastes like dates; used in puddings, cakes and bread. Not the same fruit sold in stores, but closely related. Often in mixed forests. Shade tolerant and slow growing, it can live in understory for many years. Close-grained, hard and strong wood is used for billiard cues. One of two native members of the Ebony family in the U.S., which includes more than 450 species around the world, mostly in tropical areas. Also called Simmon or Possumwood.

thorn

bark

flower

fruit

Osage-orange
Maclura pomifera

Family: Mulberry (Moraceae)

Height: 30–40' (9–12 m)

Tree: small to medium tree with a short, often crooked trunk, many spreading branches, irregular crown

Leaf: simple, oval, 3–5" (7.5–12.5 cm) long, alternately attached, long pointed tip, round to heart-shaped at base, a smooth, often wavy margin, no teeth, shiny dark green above, lighter below and lacking hairs, thorns, 1" (2.5 cm) long, at the leaf base

Bark: gray to brown with narrow forking ridges, orange inner bark where bark has been removed

Flower: clusters of green-to-cream flowers, 1" (2.5 cm) wide, on a thin fruit stalk, 2–3" (5–7.5 cm) long

Fruit: large, hard, fleshy, grainy balls, 3–5" (7.5–12.5 cm) wide, milky sap, many small brown seeds

Fall Color: yellow

Origin/Age: non-native; 100–200 years

Habitat: deep rich soils, moist soils, river valleys, sun

Range: planted in parks and yards, along streets, as windbreaks and hedgerows

Stan's Notes: An ornamental tree named after Osage Indians, who made bows and clubs from the wood, and its dimpled fruit, whose skin resembles that of an orange. Also called Horse Apple, Hedge Apple or Mock Orange. Planted around homesteads before barbed wire was available, thorns (see inset) serving as fences. Wood is durable, but not used commercially. Yellow substance from roots was used to dye clothing and baskets. This was the first tree sample Lewis and Clark sent back from the Louisiana Territory in 1804. The oldest living tree is estimated to be 330 years old in Virginia.

bark

flower

fruit

Witch-hazel
Hamamelis virginiana

SIMPLE
ALTERNATE

Family: Witch-hazel (Hamamelidaceae)

Height: 20–30' (6–9 m)

Tree: small tree, multiple thin trunks are often crooked, spreading branches, broad open crown

Leaf: simple, oval to round, 3–6" (7.5–15 cm) in length, alternately attached, with pointed or rounded tip, asymmetrical base, irregular wavy margin, coarse teeth, dark green above, slightly lighter below

Bark: light brown, smooth, uniform, sometimes scaly

Flower: bright yellow flower, 4 long, thin, twisted petals, in clusters of 3, located at joint where leaf attaches to twig, blooms in autumn

Fruit: green capsule, turning orange and splitting open at maturity (autumn of the following year), ¾–1" (2–2.5 cm) long, has 2 small shiny black seeds

Fall Color: yellow

Origin/Age: native; 30–50 years

Habitat: moist soils, understory of deciduous forests, shade

Range: throughout

Stan's Notes: The name "Witch" in Witch Hazel doesn't refer to witchcraft, but comes from an old English word "Wice" referring to a plant with bendable branches. "Hazel" comes from the leaves, which resemble those of the hazel shrub (*Corylus* spp.). Leaves, twigs and bark are aromatic and have been used as an astringent in medicinal washes. This species has an unusual flowering time: in the fall. Fruit develops the following summer and matures in autumn. Capsules remain on the tree for several years even after the seeds drop to the ground.

fruit

bark

flower

Loblolly Bay
Gordonia lasianthus

Family: Tea (Theaceae)

Height: 40–60' (12–18 m)

Tree: medium-sized tree with a narrow spire-like shape, single straight trunk, pointed crown

Leaf: simple, lance-shaped, 3–6" (7.5–15 cm) long, alternately attached, narrowest at leafstalk, blunt tip, fine-toothed margin, thick and leathery, evergreen, dark green above, paler with greenish hairs below

Bark: reddish brown, thick, deep fissures, flat ridges

Flower: large 5-petaled, cup-shaped white flower with a yellow center, 2½" (6 cm) wide, on a long stalk, fragrant scent

Fruit: 5-parted green capsule, turning gray and woody at maturity, ovate, ½–¾" (1–2 cm) long, splitting open along 5 lines in fall and releasing winged seeds

Fall Color: green, leaves turning red individually year-round

Origin/Age: native; 100–150 years

Habitat: wet soils, near wetlands and swamps, along rivers and wet places, sun to partial shade

Range: eastern half of the Carolinas

Stan's Notes: A handsome, tall, narrow tree. Its evergreen leaves turn red individually before falling throughout the year. Showy flowers attract many insects and some bird species. Although naturally found in wet places, can also be cultivated in yards and gardens if watered during drought conditions. Sometimes found growing with Sweetbay (pg. 145), which has whitish hairs on underside of leaves compared to green hairs on Loblolly Bay. Genus name *Gordonia* is for British nurseryman James Gordon (1728–1791). About 70 species in this genus, but Loblolly Bay is the only one in North America.

bark

flower

Carolina Basswood
Tilia americana var. *caroliniana*

Family: Linden (Malvaceae)

Height: 40–60' (12–18 m)

Tree: single trunk, may have many trunks growing from a common point on the ground, irregular round crown with ascending branches

Leaf: simple, heart-shaped, 3–7" (7.5–18 cm) long, alternately attached, with an asymmetrical leaf base, sharp-toothed margin, dark green above, lighter green below with light brown hairs

Bark: light gray color and smooth when young, darkens with long, narrow flat-topped ridges dividing into a short block with age, inner bark fibrous

Flower: creamy yellow flower, 1–2" (2.5–5 cm) wide, in clusters of 8–14 on a long stalk, 1–2" (2.5–5 cm) long, fragrant scent

Fruit: nut-like green fruit, turning yellow when mature, round, ¼" (.6 cm) diameter, covered with light brown hairs, on a 1–2" (2.5–5 cm) long fruit stalk, hanging in clusters from a leaf-like wing

Fall Color: yellow

Origin/Age: native; 100–150 years

Habitat: moist soils, river bottoms, creeks, shade to sun

Range: throughout the Carolinas, planted in parks and yards

Stan's Notes: The most southern basswood species, found in moist valleys below 2,000 feet (610 m) of elevation. Like other basswoods, when the main tree dies or is cut, many suckering trees quickly grow from the base. Its smooth-grained soft wood is used for carving. Inner bark was used to make mats, rope and baskets. Once thought to be a subspecies of American Basswood (pg. 191). Also called Basswood or American Linden. Its flowers are a favorite of honey bees.

bark

flower

fruit

American Basswood
Tilia americana

Family: Linden (Malvaceae)

Height: 50–70' (15–21 m)

Tree: tall tree, single or multiple trunks from a common point on the ground, full round crown

Leaf: simple, heart-shaped, 3–7" (7.5–18 cm) in length, alternately attached, with asymmetrical leaf base, sharp-toothed margin, dull green above, lighter green below

Bark: light gray color and smooth when young, darkens with long, narrow flat-topped ridges dividing into a short block with age, inner bark fibrous

Flower: creamy yellow flower, 1–2" (2.5–5 cm) diameter, fragrant scent

Fruit: nut-like green fruit, turning yellow when mature, round, ¼" (.6 cm) diameter, covered with light brown hairs, on a 1–2" (2.5–5 cm) long fruit stalk, hanging in clusters from a leaf-like wing

Fall Color: yellow to orange

Origin/Age: native; 150–200 years

Habitat: moist soils, partial shade to sun

Range: throughout

Stan's Notes: A long-lived, fast-growing tree that is well known for growing several trunks from the base of the mother plant. The light-weight soft wood is used for carving due to its smooth grain. From its flowers, bees produce a high quality honey. Fibrous inner bark was once used by American Indians to weave mats, rope and baskets. Also called American Linden or Basswood. White Basswood, once considered its own species, is now believed to be a variety of the American Basswood. Many cultivated varieties exist.

bark

fruit

cross section

Sycamore
Platanus occidentalis

SIMPLE ALTERNATE

Family: Sycamore (Platanaceae)

Height: 60–90' (18–27.5 m)

Tree: large tree, often a single massive trunk, enlarged at the base, open widely spreading crown

Leaf: simple, triangular, 4–8" (10–20 cm) in length, alternately attached, 3–5 shallow pointed lobes, wavy coarse-toothed margin, 3 prominent veins, bright green above, paler below

Bark: pale white color, smooth, peeling off in large thin sections, green and cream-to-white inner bark produces a mottled effect, bark on the base of tree often much darker than upper bark

Fruit: light brown round aggregate of many nutlets, 1" (2.5 cm) in diameter, hanging from a long fruit stalk, remaining on tree into winter

Fall Color: brown

Origin/Age: native; 200–250 years

Habitat: moist soils, rich bottomlands, sun to partial shade

Range: throughout

Stan's Notes: One of the largest broadleaf trees in the Carolinas. Produces a massive white trunk, larger in diameter than many other trees in the two states, which makes it easy to identify. Its branches are often crooked, making this species easy to climb. Some hollow trunks of large old trees are used by many animals and birds as homes. It is a fast-growing tree that usually grows in old fields or along streams. Often planted as an ornamental tree in landscapes or parks. Also called American Sycamore, American Plane Tree or Buttonball-tree. Of the ten sycamore species, only three are found in the U.S. and Canada.

bark

flower

fruit

Sourwood
Oxydendrum arboreum

SIMPLE ALTERNATE

Family: Heath (Ericaceae)

Height: 30–50' (9–15 m)

Tree: slender pyramid shape, crooked or leaning trunk, short horizontal branches, narrow crown

Leaf: simple, lance-shaped, 5–10" (12.5–25 cm) long, alternately attached, narrow pointed tip, fine-toothed margin, glossy yellow-green above and paler below

Bark: rusty brown, smooth when young, turning rough and furrowed with broad ridges with age

Flower: many small, bell-shaped white flowers, ⅓" (.8 cm) wide, made of 5 petals, hanging on a stalk, up to 12" (30 cm) long, in large clusters, fragrant

Fruit: many small dry green capsules, turning gray at maturity, ½" (1 cm) long, splitting along 5 seams in autumn and releasing seeds, remaining on tree well into winter

Fall Color: scarlet red to purple

Origin/Age: native; 50–100 years

Habitat: variety of soils from moist to dry, river valleys, exposed hillsides, sun to partial shade

Range: throughout, planted in parks and yards

Stan's Notes: Large drooping clusters of fragrant white flowers in spring and summer, scarlet red leaves in fall and seedpods in winter make this an attractive tree year-round. Has been planted as an ornamental in yards. Genus name is Greek, with *Oxy* for "acid" or "sharp" and *dendron* for "tree." The leaves have a sour taste. Related to blueberries (*Vaccinium* spp.). Native of the southeastern U.S.

bark

flower

fruit

Pawpaw
Asimina triloba

Family: Custard-apple (Annonaceae)

Height: 20–30' (6–9 m)

Tree: understory tree, single or multiple straight trunks, straight branches, broad crown

Leaf: simple, obovate, 7–10" (18–25 cm) long, alternately attached, widest near the tip, smooth toothless margin, medium green above, paler below, short leafstalk (petiole)

Bark: brown, smooth, thin, covered with tiny bumps

Flower: triangular flower, 1–2" (2.5–5 cm) wide, made of 6 reddish purple petals, solitary or in small clusters, nodding on stalk, unpleasant odor

Fruit: green berry-like fruit, turning yellow to brown or black at maturity, soft edible flesh with prune-like texture and fruity custard flavor, round to slightly curved, 3–5" (7.5–12.5 cm) long, single or in small clusters, several large seeds, ½" (1 cm) wide

Fall Color: yellow

Origin/Age: native; 100–150 years

Habitat: moist soils, floodplains, shade

Range: throughout, planted in parks and yards

Stan's Notes: An unusual tree with large leaves and tiny banana-shaped fruit. Also known as Wild Banana or Appalachian Banana. In a mostly tropical tree family that produces fruit such as soursops and custard apples. New shoots grow from roots, forming large dense thickets or colonies. Flowers appear with leaves. Fruit was eaten by American Indians and early settlers and is sold in some stores today.

bark

flower

fruit

American Chestnut
Castanea dentata

Family: Beech (Fagaceae)

Height: 60–90' (18–27.5 m)

Tree: once a tall tree growing to 115' (35 m), but now rarely reaching maturity due to chestnut blight, full round crown

Leaf: simple, narrow, 6–12" (15–30 cm) in length, alternately attached, tapering at each end, with unique prominent teeth that extend beyond leaf margin and form a forward curve like the teeth of a saw, straight and parallel veins

Bark: dark brown to red, smooth, separating into wide flat-topped ridges

Flower: catkin with male and female flowers on same tree (monoecious), male flower in catkin, 1" (2.5 cm) long, solitary female flower, ½" (1 cm) wide, located at base of the catkin

Fruit: bur-like green nut, turning brown at maturity, 2–3" (5–7.5 cm) wide, in clusters, splits into 4 parts

Fall Color: yellow

Origin/Age: native; 25–50 years

Habitat: well-drained sandy soils, sun

Range: western quarter of the Carolinas

Stan's Notes: There are three chestnut species in North America, with this one producing the proverbial chestnuts roasting over an open fire. Once a large and prominent tree of the eastern U.S., it was nearly wiped out by chestnut blight, a fungus. Grows to half its former size before dying. Hard oak-like wood with a straight grain, relatively decay resistant. Will sprout from stumps of dead or cut trees. The species name *dentata* refers to the obvious large teeth on leaves.

bark

flower

fruit

Amur Maple
Acer ginnala

Family: Maple (Aceraceae)

Height: 15–20' (4.5–6 m)

Tree: small tree, trunk often multi-stemmed, compact lower branches, irregular crown

Leaf: lobed, arrowhead-shaped, 2–4" (5–10 cm) in length, oppositely attached, with 3–5 sharp lobes, coarse teeth, glossy green, leafstalk often bright red

Bark: gray, smooth with many vertical cracks

Flower: small green flower, ½" (1 cm) wide, in drooping clusters, 1–2" (2.5–5 cm) wide

Fruit: pair of red-tinged winged seeds (samara), turning bright red, 1–2" (2.5–5 cm) long

Fall Color: red to orange

Origin/Age: non-native, introduced to the U.S. from eastern Asia; 25–50 years

Habitat: well-drained soils, shade

Range: planted in parks and yards

Stan's Notes: A remarkably attractive small tree, widely planted as an ornamental shrub for its brilliance in autumn. Very hardy, shade-tolerant plant that turns a showy bright red each fall, with winged seeds (samara) also turning bright red. The samaras are often called helicopters due to the way they rotate to the ground. The genus name *Acer* is Latin and means "sharp," referring to its pointed lobes. The common name comes from the Amur River, which forms the boundary between China and Russia, presumably the origin of this species. Also called Siberian Maple.

bark

flower

fruit

Mountain Maple
Acer spicatum

Family: Maple (Aceraceae)

Height: 20–30' (6–9 m)

Tree: small tree with a single crooked trunk and upright branches, irregular crown

Leaf: lobed, 2–4" (5–10 cm) long, oppositely attached, 3 pointed lobes (rarely 5), coarse-toothed margin, light green, leafstalk often red, usually longer than the leaf

Bark: reddish to brown, smooth but grooved with light-colored areas

Flower: many 5-petaled yellowish green flowers, each ½" (1 cm) diameter, growing in spike clusters, 1–3" (2.5–7.5 cm) tall

Fruit: pair of winged seeds (samara), often red, turning yellow, then brown, ¾–1" (2–2.5 cm) long

Fall Color: red or orange

Origin/Age: native; 40–60 years

Habitat: moist soils, along streams and other wet areas, shade tolerant

Range: western quarter of North Carolina, planted in parks and yards

Stan's Notes: Usually is considered an understory tree because it commonly grows under the canopy of larger, more dominant trees. Doesn't do well in the open. Often grows in rocky outcroppings. The winged seeds are often bright red, later turning yellow, then brown in late summer before falling in early winter. Shallow root system. The wood hasn't been considered for any commercial use.

bark

fruit

Southern Sugar Maple
Acer saccharum var. saccharum

Family: Maple (Aceraceae)

Height: 40–60' (12–18 m)

Tree: single straight trunk, many ascending branches, narrow pointed crown

Leaf: lobed, 2–3½" (5–9 cm) long, oppositely attached, 3–5 short lobes, smooth margin or with a few coarse teeth, dark green above, paler with fine hairs below

Bark: light gray to white, smooth, becoming furrowed with age

Fruit: pair of green winged seeds (samara), turning tan, ¾–2" (2–5 cm) long

Fall Color: yellow and red

Origin/Age: native; 100–150 years

Habitat: rich moist soils in a wide variety of habitats, along streams and rivers, valleys, sun

Range: throughout the Carolinas

Stan's Notes: Closely related to the Sugar Maple (*A. saccharum*), which is scattered in the Carolinas. Hybridizes with Sugar Maple where their ranges overlap. The Southern Sugar Maple is considered a subspecies or variety of Sugar Maple, with smaller leaves. Southern Sugar Maple can be tapped to gather sap for making maple syrup, but it is reported to have significantly less flow than Sugar Maple. However, to get sap to flow in the tree, night time temperatures need to be below freezing and daytime temperatures above, so therefore they are not tapped for sap. In the Carolinas most grow to 60 feet (18 m) tall. Also called Florida Sugar Maple.

bark

flower

fruit

Red Maple
Acer rubrum

Family: Maple (Aceraceae)

Height: 40–60' (12–18 m)

Tree: single trunk, narrow dense crown

Leaf: lobed, 3–4" (7.5–10 cm) long, oppositely attached, 3–5 lobes (usually 3), shallow notches in between lobes, double-toothed margin, light green color, red leafstalk

Bark: gray, smooth, broken by narrow irregular cracks

Flower: tiny red hanging flower, ¼" (.6 cm) wide, on a 1–2" (2.5–5 cm) long red stalk, growing in clusters, 1–3" (2.5–7.5 cm) wide

Fruit: pair of winged seeds (samara), red in springtime, ½–1" (1–2.5 cm) long

Fall Color: red to orange

Origin/Age: native; 75–100 years

Habitat: wet to moist soils, along swamps or depressions that hold water, sun to partial shade

Range: throughout

Stan's Notes: One of the most drought-tolerant species of maple in the Carolinas. Often planted as an ornamental, it can be identified by its characteristic leaves, which have three pointed lobes, and red stalks. The common name comes from the obvious red flowers that bloom early in spring, but the flowers and leafstalks are not the only red colors it has. New leaves, fall color and spring seeds are also red. Produces one of the smallest seeds of any of the maples. Also called Swamp Maple, Water Maple or Soft Maple, the latter being used to refer to the Silver Maple (pg. 213) as well. Even though it is sometimes called Soft Maple, its wood is very hard and brittle.

bark

flower

fruit

Sugar Maple
Acer saccharum

LOBED OPPOSITE

Family: Maple (Aceraceae)

Height: 50–70' (15–21 m)

Tree: single trunk, ascending branches, narrow round to oval crown

Leaf: lobed, 3–5" (7.5–12.5 cm) in length, oppositely attached, 5 lobes (occasionally 3), pointed tips, few irregular teeth, wavy margin, yellowish green above, paler below

Bark: gray in color, narrow furrows and irregular ridges, can be scaly

Flower: greenish yellow flower, ¼" (.6 cm) wide, dangling on a 1–2" (2.5–5 cm) long stalk

Fruit: pair of green winged seeds (samara), turning tan, ¾–1½" (2–4 cm) long

Fall Color: orange to red

Origin/Age: native; 150–200 years

Habitat: rich moist soils, sun

Range: western quarter of North Carolina, planted in yards, parks and along roads

Stan's Notes: A popular and well-known tree, Sugar Maples are the source of maple syrup and maple sugar. It takes approximately 40 gallons (152 L) of sap to make a single gallon of syrup. Any break in a twig, branch or trunk leaks sugary water in spring, attracting birds, bugs and mammals, which lap up the sap. Leaves that have fallen break down quickly, making it one of the best natural and organic fertilizers. Also known as Hard Maple, its extremely hard wood is used in furniture, flooring and cabinets. Often planted in yards and parks and along roads. This species closely resembles the Black Maple (pg. 211).

bark

fruit

Black Maple
Acer nigrum

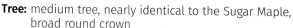

Family: Maple (Aceraceae)

Height: 40–70' (12–21 m)

Tree: medium tree, nearly identical to the Sugar Maple, broad round crown

Leaf: lobed, 3–6" (7.5–15 cm) long, oppositely attached, 3 pointed lobes (rarely 5), with a smooth to wavy margin, dark green above, yellowish below, leaves appear to droop

Bark: light gray, smooth, can get scaly with age

Fruit: pair of green winged seeds (samara), turning tan, 1–2" (2.5–5 cm) long

Fall Color: yellow

Origin/Age: native; 150–175 years

Habitat: moist fertile soils, floodplains, bottomlands, shade

Range: western quarter of North Carolina, planted in parks and yards

Stan's Notes: Nearly identical to the Sugar Maple (pg. 209), with several areas of differentiation. Common name "Black" refers to its bark, which is not black but often is darker than Sugar Maple bark. Leaves occasionally have dense, velvety brownish hairs underneath. They sometimes also have a characteristic wilted appearance and turn yellow in fall rather than red, like Sugar Maple leaves. Black Maple trees grow in moister soils and are more drought tolerant and slower growing than Sugar Maples, but they breed easily with each other. Seeds laying in soil remain viable for many years.

underside

bark

flower

fruit

Silver Maple
Acer saccharinum

Family: Maple (Aceraceae)

Height: 75–100' (23–30.5 m)

Tree: single trunk, ascending branches, open crown

Leaf: lobed, 4–6" (10–15 cm) long, oppositely attached, 5–7 lobes, pointed tips, deep notches and double-toothed margin, dull green above with a silvery white color below

Bark: gray and smooth when young, becomes furrowed, long scaly strips, often peeling and curling at ends

Flower: tiny red dangling flower, ¼" (.6 cm) wide, on 1–2" (2.5–5 cm) long stalk

Fruit: pair of green winged seeds (samara), turning to brown, 1–2½" (2.5–6 cm) long

Fall Color: yellow to orange

Origin/Age: native; 100–125 years

Habitat: wet to moist soils, often growing in pure stands in floodplains, shade

Range: western half of the Carolinas, planted in parks and yards

Stan's Notes: Usually seen growing in bottomlands or floodplains along rivers, where it is often the dominant tree. This is one of the first trees to bloom (flower) in spring, confusing many to think it is budding early. Bark of older trees is characteristic, with long strips that often peel and curl at ends. Produces heavy seed crops. Also called Silver-leaf Maple for the silvery appearance of the underside of leaves, and Soft Maple, which is also another name of the Red Maple (pg. 207). This name refers to the brittle branches (which often break off in windstorms), rather than to the wood being soft. The wood is actually very hard with a tight grain.

bark

flower

fruit

Striped Maple
Acer pensylvanicum

Family: Maple (Aceraceae)

Height: 10–30' (3–9 m)

Tree: single or multiple crooked trunks, many short thin branches, open conical or flat crown

Leaf: lobed, 5–7" (12.5–18 cm) in length, oppositely attached, with 3 short pointed lobes near the tip, occasionally without lobes, sharp-toothed margin, 3 main veins extend from the leaf base to the end of each lobe, light green above, paler below, stout leafstalk, 2–2½" (5–6 cm) long

Bark: green with vertical white stripes, becoming darker with age

Flower: many 5-petaled, bell-shaped yellow flowers, ⅜" (.9 cm) long, on a long stalk, hanging vertically

Fruit: pair of winged seeds (samara), 1¼" (3 cm) long

Fall Color: yellow

Origin/Age: native; 50–75 years

Habitat: moist upland soils, understory of forests, shade

Range: western quarter of the Carolinas, planted in parks and yards

Stan's Notes: A small ornamental tree, often confused with a shrub. Easy to identify, even in winter, by its unique striped bark. If pruned it will develop with a single trunk, but if left unchecked it will grow with many trunks. Grows in the shade of other larger trees in the forest. White-tailed Deer browse on the leaves in spring and summer and twigs and saplings in winter.

fruit

bark

flower

Norway Maple
Acer platanoides

Family: Maple (Aceraceae)

Height: 40–60' (12–18 m)

Tree: single straight trunk, dense round crown

Leaf: lobed, 5–7" (12.5–18 cm) in length, oppositely attached, 5–7 lobes, shallow notches and a wavy margin, exudes milky sap when cut, shiny dark green above, light green below

Bark: dark gray in color with many narrow furrows and interlacing ridges

Flower: large green flower, ½–¾" (1–2 cm) wide, on a 1–2" (2.5–5 cm) long green stalk

Fruit: pair of widely spread winged seeds (samara), 1–2" (2.5–5 cm) long

Fall Color: yellow to orange

Origin/Age: non-native, introduced to the U.S. from Europe; 100–125 years

Habitat: well-drained rich soils, sun to partial shade

Range: planted in parks, yards and along streets

Stan's Notes: This introduced species, most commonly seen along streets and in parks, has spread to wild environments and is doing well. Considered to be one of the most disease- and insect-resistant species of maple and a potential species that could outperform the widely prevalent native maples. While leaves are similar to those of Sugar Maple (pg. 209), several Norway Maple varieties have red or purple leaves. Leaves, buds and twigs exude a milky sap when cut. Winged seeds are more widely spread than those of Sugar Maple or Silver Maple (pg. 213). Common name implies it was introduced from Norway.

underside

bark

flower

fruit

White Poplar
Populus alba

LOBED
ALTERNATE

Family: Willow (Salicaceae)

Height: 40–60' (12–18 m)

Tree: medium-sized tree with single or multiple trunks, open widely spreading crown

Leaf: lobed, maple-shaped, 2–5" (5–12.5 cm) in length, alternately attached, 3 pointed lobes, few rounded teeth, light green above and chalky white below, covered with white hairs, silky white when young

Bark: dark brown color and deeply furrowed near base, yellowish white color with dark horizontal marks (lenticels) and smooth upper

Flower: catkin, 2–3" (5–7.5 cm) long, composed of many tiny flowers, ¼" (.6 cm) wide

Fruit: catkin-like fruit, 2–3" (5–7.5 cm) long, composed of many capsules that open and release many tiny cottony seeds, which float on the wind

Fall Color: yellow to brown

Origin/Age: non-native, introduced to the U.S. from Europe; 100–125 years

Habitat: wide variety of soils, sun

Range: planted in parks, yards and along roads

Stan's Notes: The maple-like lobed leaves of the White Poplar are unusual for a member of the *Populus* genus. Buds and leaf undersides are covered with tiny white hairs, giving newly budded leaves a whitish-colored appearance and the species its common name. Also known as Silver-leaf Poplar or European White Poplar, it was among the first trees that were introduced to North America from Europe during colonial times. A fast-growing tree with several varieties sold. Species name *alba* means "white."

bark

flower

fruit

Sassafras
Sassafras albidum

Family: Laurel (Lauraceae)

Height: 30–60' (9–18 m)

Tree: medium-sized columnar tree with single crooked trunk, branches often crooked and spreading, flat irregular crown

Leaf: lobed or simple, 3–5" (7.5–12.5 cm) in length, alternately attached, often has 1, 2 or 3 lobes with mitten-shaped 1-lobed leaves, simple elliptical leaves along with lobed leaves appear on the same tree, smooth toothless margin, shiny green above, paler below and often hairy

Bark: brown, deeply furrowed with age

Flower: green-to-yellow flower, ¼" (.6 cm) wide, on a 1–2" (2.5–5 cm) long stalk, in clusters

Fruit: blue-to-nearly-black fruit (drupe), ½" (1 cm) wide, on a 1" (2.5 cm) long fruit stalk, in clusters, each containing 1 seed

Fall Color: yellow to red

Origin/Age: native; 100–150 years

Habitat: moist and dry soils, forest edges, sun to partial sun

Range: throughout

Stan's Notes: Like other laurels, crushed leaves and twigs have a spicy fragrance. Its shallow roots once supplied oil of sassafras for perfuming soap. Once thought to have medicinal properties, the settlers brewed its bark and roots into a tea. A compound in Sassafras is suspected to be a carcinogen as is banned as a food additive. One of our first exports. Has an American Indian name. Produces dense cover and fruit for wildlife. Sometimes planted as an ornamental for its fall colors and fruit. Soft wood breaks easily.

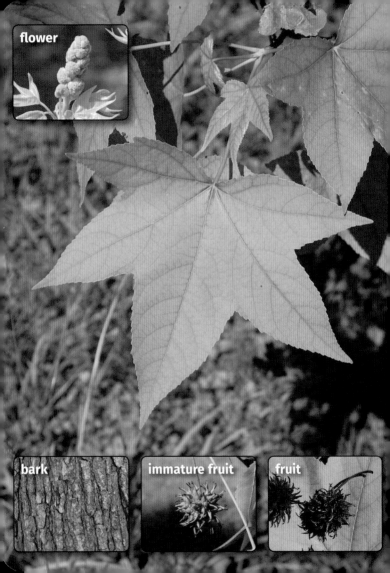

flower

bark

immature fruit

fruit

Sweetgum
Liquidambar styraciflua

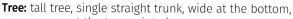

Family: Witch-hazel (Altingiaceae)

Height: 80–100' (24.5–30.5 m)

Tree: tall tree, single straight trunk, wide at the bottom, narrow at the top, pointed crown

Leaf: lobed, 3–6" (7.5–15 cm) long, alternately attached, star-shaped, 5–7 long pointed lobes, fine-toothed, 5 main veins from a notched base to tip of each lobe, shiny dark green above, whitish green below

Bark: gray to brown, deeply furrowed into narrow scales

Flower: ball-shaped green flower, ½–¾" (1–2 cm) wide, in clusters, on a 1–2" (2.5–5 cm) drooping stalk

Fruit: round green cluster, 1–1½" (2.5–4 cm) diameter, turns brown at maturity, many hard woody spines, on a long fruit stalk, has many flat, winged seeds

Fall Color: red

Origin/Age: native; 100–150 years

Habitat: moist soils, river valleys, mixed woods, old fields

Range: throughout

Stan's Notes: Often planted as a shade tree and for its bright red leaves in fall. Can be in pure stands, but usually grows with other deciduous trees. Moderately rapid growing. Matures at 20–25 years. Flowers in spring. Fruit matures in fall and opens to release seeds. Seeds eaten by birds and animals. Old fruit may stay on the tree in winter. Is an important tree commercially, surpassed only by oaks. Dark reddish brown, hard, heavy wood is used for furniture veneer, plywood and barrels. Well known for its resin, obtained by peeling back bark and scraping it off. The gum has been used medicinally, in soaps and in adhesives and for chewing gum. The leaves are aromatic if crushed.

bark

flower

fruit

Tulip-tree
Liriodendron tulipifera

Family: Magnolia (Magnoliaceae)

Height: 80–100' (24.5–30.5 m)

Tree: large tree, single straight trunk, branch-free lower half, ascending upper branches, drooping lower branches, narrow crown

Leaf: lobed, 3–6" (7.5–15 cm) long, alternately attached, unusual shapes, some nearly square but most with 4–6 pointed lobes, shiny green above, paler below, smooth toothless margin, very long leafstalk

Bark: gray, deeply furrowed with age

Flower: large, showy, tulip-shaped flower, 1–2" (2.5–5 cm) long, made of 6 yellow petals with orange bases

Fruit: green aggregate, turning light brown at maturity, cone-shaped, 3" (7.5 cm) long, growing upright on branch, containing tiny winged nutlets that fall apart in autumn and release seeds

Fall Color: yellow

Origin/Age: native; 100–150 years

Habitat: moist soils, along streams, ponds and other wet places, sun

Range: throughout

Stan's Notes: Often one of the tallest trees in the forest. Also called Yellow Poplar due to the heartwood color, but it is not a poplar. Two *Liriodendron* species, one in China. Fossil evidence shows these trees were once found throughout much more of the northern hemisphere. Its colorful flowers give it the common name. Fast growing, with some reaching nearly 200 feet (61 m). Loses its lower leaves as it develops. A tonic from its bitter, aromatic roots was used for heart ailments.

bark

fruit

Blackjack Oak
Quercus marilandica

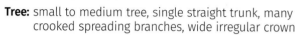

Family: Beech (Fagaceae)

Height: 25–40' (7.5–12 m)

Tree: small to medium tree, single straight trunk, many crooked spreading branches, wide irregular crown

Leaf: lobed, 2–6" (5–15 cm) long, alternately attached, 3–5 broad, shallowly divided lobes, lobes broadest at the top, each lobe bristle-tipped, leathery, waxy, shiny dark green above and dull green below with brown hairs along veins

Bark: nearly black bark that is rough, thick and deeply furrowed into nearly square plates

Fruit: green acorn, turning brown when mature, edible, oblong, ½–¾" (1–2 cm) long, with a stout pointed tip, single or in pairs on a very short stalk, cap covers the upper half of nut, matures in 2 seasons

Fall Color: brown to yellow

Origin/Age: native; 150–200 years

Habitat: dry, sandy or clay soils, often on upland ridges, sun

Range: throughout

Stan's Notes: Frequently associated with poor soils. Tolerates dry, sandy or gravelly soils where few other forest oaks live. Also called Scrub Oak due to its stunted, scrubby growth. First described in the 1770s from a tree found in Maryland, hence the species name. Club-shaped leaves give it the common name. Leaves are covered with a waxy substance (cutin) that helps reduce water loss in hot, dry environments. Retains leaves well into winter. Small acorns take two years to mature. New shoots sprout from burned or cut trunks. Wood is sometimes used for railroad ties and firewood.

bark

fruit

Water Oak
Quercus nigra

Family: Beech (Fagaceae)

Height: 50–70' (15–21 m)

Tree: medium-sized tree with a single straight trunk, tall conical crown composed of slender branches

Leaf: lobed, spatulate to wedge-shaped, 2–6" (5–15 cm) long, alternately attached, usually 1–3 round or pointed shallow lobes, widest at the tip, toothless margin, dull blue-green above, paler below, may have tufts of hair along vein angles

Bark: gray to black, thin and smooth, becoming scaly with age

Fruit: green acorn, turning nearly black when mature, ⅓–⅝" (.8–1.5 cm) long, shallow cap, nutmeat is bright orange and bitter, maturing the second year

Fall Color: yellow to brown

Origin/Age: native; 75–100 years

Habitat: moist to wet soils, along river floodplains, partial shade to full sun

Range: eastern half of the Carolinas, planted in parks, yards and along streets

Stan's Notes: Found in moist bottomland sites in and around the Carolinas. This species is unlike many other oaks, which require drier soils. Common name given because it grows in wet areas. A moderate to fast-growing tree that tolerates some shade but does best in full sun. Easy to propagate, it has been planted in city parks and along streets throughout the South. Occasionally called Spotted Oak or Possum Oak. Starts producing acorns after 20 years.

bark

fruit

Pin Oak
Quercus palustris

Family: Beech (Fagaceae)

Height: 50–70' (15–21 m)

Tree: medium-sized tree with a single trunk, drooping branches and open irregular crown

Leaf: lobed, 3–5" (7.5–12.5 cm) in length, alternately attached, 5–7 lobes, each ending in a pointed tip (bristle-tipped), deep sinuses in between the lobes cutting nearly to the midrib, shiny green above, light green below with tufts of hair along midrib

Bark: dark brown with shallow furrows and flat ridges

Flower: green-to-red catkin, 1–4" (2.5–10 cm) long, made up of many tiny flowers, ⅛" (.3 cm) wide

Fruit: green acorn, turning brown when mature, edible, ½" (1 cm) long, elongated cap covering the upper third of nut, maturing at the end of the second year

Fall Color: deep red to reddish brown

Origin/Age: native; 100–150 years

Habitat: wet soils, frequently in heavy clay, poorly drained upland sites, sun

Range: scattered locations in the western half of North Carolina, planted in parks and yards

Stan's Notes: One of over 600 species of oak in the world. Often grows in pure stands. Flowers are pollinated in the first year; acorns mature in fall of the second year. Heavy fruit crops every 4–6 years. Acorns are eaten by wildlife. Acorns contain tannic acid (tannin), which can be toxic in large amounts. Susceptible to oak wilt, a fungus that can kill entire stands of trees. Pin Oak (*Q. ellipsoidalis*) of the upper Midwest has similar leaves. Also called Spanish Oak.

bark

fruit

Post Oak
Quercus stellata

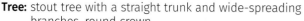

Family: Beech (Fagaceae)

Height: 30–60' (9–18 m)

Tree: stout tree with a straight trunk and wide-spreading branches, round crown

Leaf: lobed, unique shape suggests a Maltese cross, 3–7" (7.5–18 cm) long, alternately attached, 5–7 deep, squared lobes with 2 large middle lobes, rounded tip, tapered base, dark green above, paler below, leafstalk often stout and hairy, yellow star-shaped hairs on underside of leaf

Bark: light gray with scaly ridges

Fruit: green acorn, turning brown when mature, edible, egg-shaped (ovate), ½–1" (1–2.5 cm) long, single on a very short stalk or stalkless, thin cap covering the upper third of nut

Fall Color: brown

Origin/Age: native; 200–250 years

Habitat: sandy, gravelly soils, along hills and ridges, along streams and rivers in floodplains, sun

Range: throughout

Stan's Notes: A slow-growing, medium-sized oak. Drought resistant, often planted in dry rocky soils where other oaks won't survive. Frequently scrubby due to nutrient-poor soils. Unique leaf shape makes it easy to identify, but shape varies. Some leaves look like a cross. Thick yellowish twigs and star-shaped hairs on leaves help to identify. *Stellata* refers to the star shape of the leaf hairs. Wood was used for fence posts, hence the common name. Produces acorns each year, but has heavy crops every 2–4 years. An important food source for wildlife.

bark

fruit

Scarlet Oak

Quercus coccinea

Family: Beech (Fagaceae)

Height: 60–70' (18–21 m)

Tree: medium tree with a straight trunk, wide spreading branches, round crown

Leaf: lobed, 3–7" (7.5–18 cm) long, alternately attached, 5–7 pointed lobes, round sinuses, deeply divided nearly to the midrib, dark green and glossy above, paler yellowish below, leafstalk often reddish

Bark: dark gray, becoming darker with age, scaly ridges

Fruit: green acorn, turning brown when mature, edible, egg-shaped (ovate), ½–1" (1–2.5 cm) long, single on a short stalk, cap covering the upper third to half of nut, maturing in 2 seasons

Fall Color: scarlet red

Origin/Age: native; 100–150 years

Habitat: dry, sandy or gravelly soils, along hills and ridges, often with other oaks, sun

Range: western half of the Carolinas

Stan's Notes: A component of eastern deciduous forests, growing with many other oaks such as White Oak (pg. 241) and Black Oak (pg. 245). Planted in parks and yards and along streets for its form, exceptional shade and brilliant fall color, for which it was named. Drought tolerant and fast growing, this tree thrives in well-drained soils. Not as long lived as many other oaks. A red oak, producing flowers in the spring. Acorns mature at the end of the second year. Heavy acorn crops are often followed by 3–4 years with few or no acorns. Lumber is marketed as Red Oak but is not as desirable as White Oak wood.

bark

fruit

Shumard Oak
Quercus shumardii

Family: Beech (Fagaceae)

Height: 60–90' (18–27.5 m)

Tree: large tree, single straight trunk, wide round crown

Leaf: lobed, 3–7" (7.5–18 cm) long, alternately attached, 5–9 pointed lobes, round sinuses, deeply divided nearly to the midrib, broadest at the top, several bristle-tipped teeth, dark green above, dull green below with tufts of hair at vein angles

Bark: gray, becoming darker with age, shallow furrows

Fruit: green acorn, turning brown when mature, edible, egg-shaped (ovate), ¾–1¼" (2–3 cm) long, single or in pairs on a short stalk, cap covering the upper third to half of nut, maturing in 2 seasons

Fall Color: red to brown

Origin/Age: native; 150–200 years

Habitat: moist soils along rivers, streams and swamps or scattered in deciduous forests and river valleys

Range: throughout

Stan's Notes: A larger oak in North America, some growing nearly 100 feet (30.5) tall, with a very wide crown. Grows the best in well-drained soils along rivers. Usually is considered an oak of the Deep South, where it is planted as an ornamental tree. Hybridizes with other oak species, especially Shingle Oak (pg. 125) and Blackjack Oak (pg. 227), making them hard to distinguish. Often substituted for Scarlet Oak (pg. 235). Moderately fast-growing tree that flowers in spring. Acorns mature in the fall of its second year. Very large acorn crops every 4–6 years. Wood has been used for flooring, veneers and furniture. Sold as Red Oak. Named for B. F. Shumard, state geologist of Texas in the mid-1800s.

bark

flower

fruit

Swamp White Oak
Quercus bicolor

Family: Beech (Fagaceae)

Height: 40–60' (12–18 m)

Tree: single trunk, crooked lower branches and narrow irregular crown

Leaf: lobed, 4–7" (10–18 cm) long, alternately attached, widest above the middle, with shallow lobes that occasionally appear like teeth, dark green above, paler below with white hairs, obvious difference between upper and lower leaf surfaces

Bark: light gray, many vertical furrows, wide flat ridges

Flower: thin catkin, 1–4" (2.5–10 cm) long, composed of hairy green flowers

Fruit: green acorn, turning brown when mature, edible, ¾–1¼" (2–3 cm) long, single but can be in pairs, knobby cap covering the upper half of nut

Fall Color: brown

Origin/Age: native; 150–200 years

Habitat: moist soils, along river bottoms, wetland edges

Range: scattered locations in North Carolina

Stan's Notes: This is a common, fast-growing oak of moist soils. Its acorns, which mature in one season and usually grow in pairs on a long stalk, sprout soon after they fall from the tree in late summer and autumn. Leaf lobes are shallow, unlike the deeply lobed leaves typical of other members of the white oak group such as the White Oak (pg. 241). Also called Bicolor Oak (from the species name *bicolor*), which refers to its distinctly different upper and lower leaf surfaces. The crooked lower branches tend to hang down, giving it a messy appearance. Does very well as a landscape plant. Its hard, durable wood has been used in making furniture.

fruit

bark

flower

White Oak
Quercus alba

LOBED
ALTERNATE

Family: Beech (Fagaceae)

Height: 50–70' (15–21 m)

Tree: single straight trunk, some gnarled and twisted branches reach toward the ground, broad crown

Leaf: lobed, 4–8" (10–20 cm) long, alternately attached, 5–9 rounded lobes, notches deeply cut or shallow and uniform in size and depth, often widest above middle, lacking teeth, bright green above, paler below, leaves often clustered at ends of branches

Bark: light gray, broken into reddish scales

Flower: green catkin, 1–3" (2.5–7.5 cm) long, composed of many tiny flowers, ⅛" (.3 cm) wide

Fruit: green acorn, turns brown, edible, ½–1½" (1–4 cm) long, cap covers the upper third of nut

Fall Color: red brown

Origin/Age: native; 150–250 years

Habitat: variety of soils, sun

Range: throughout

Stan's Notes: A very important tree in the lumber industry, with its wood used for furniture, flooring, whiskey barrels, crates and much more. Produces edible acorns each fall, with large crops produced every 4–10 years. Like all other acorns, these should be boiled in several changes of water to leech out the bitter and slightly toxic tannins before eating. Acorns are an important food source for turkeys, squirrels, grouse, deer and other wildlife. Susceptible to oak wilt, causing gradual death. Oaks in the white oak group can be treated for oak wilt, while red oak group trees die quickly from the disease.

bark

fruit

Turkey Oak
Quercus laevis

Family: Beech (Fagaceae)

Height: 20–40' (6–12 m)

Tree: small to medium tree, sometimes appearing like a shrub, single straight trunk, crooked branches, open round crown

Leaf: lobed, 4–9" (10–22.5 cm) long, alternately attached, 3–5 narrow lobes, each ending in 1–3 pointed tips (bristle-tipped), thick and often stiff, shiny yellowish green above, paler with a few tufts of red hair below

Bark: dark brown to nearly black, thick, deeply furrowed with scaly ridges

Fruit: green acorn, turning brown at maturity, bitter, ovate, ¾–1" (2–2.5 cm) long, on a short stalk, cap covering the upper third to half of nut, maturing in 2 seasons

Fall Color: red to brown

Origin/Age: native; 100–125 years

Habitat: sandy soils, dunes, sometimes in pure stands, sun

Range: along the coast of the Carolinas

Stan's Notes: A small and moderately fast-growing but short-lived oak. Usually found in sandy soils along the coast. Frequently occurs in pure stands, but often associated with Longleaf Pine (pg. 47) and other oaks. Also called Catesby Oak or Scrub Oak, the latter name referring to its short scrubby growth. Has never been used commercially due to its small size. Its small bitter acorns mature in two seasons and are eaten by wildlife, such as Black Bear, White-tailed Deer and turkeys. Hybridizes with Southern Red Oak (pg. 249), Laurel Oak (pg. 123) and Water Oak (pg. 229).

bark

fruit

Black Oak
Quercus velutina

LOBED
ALTERNATE

Family: Beech (Fagaceae)

Height: 40–60' (12–18 m)

Tree: medium-sized tree, lower branches are ascending before maturity and horizontal at maturity, upper branches ascending, broad round crown

Leaf: lobed, 4–9" (10–22.5 cm) long, alternately attached, 5–7 lobes, each ending in a pointed tip (bristle-tipped) and separated by deep U-shaped sinuses, shiny green above, yellowish brown below

Bark: shiny dark gray and smooth texture when young, becoming nearly black with deep reddish cracks

Flower: light yellow catkin, 1–3" (2.5–7.5 cm) long, made up of many tiny flowers, ⅛" (.3 cm) wide

Fruit: green acorn, turns brown at maturity, ¾" (2 cm) long, almost as wide as long, thin black vertical lines on hull, cap covers the upper half of nut

Fall Color: orange-brown

Origin/Age: native; 175–200 years

Habitat: dry sandy soils, steep slopes, sun

Range: throughout

Stan's Notes: One of approximately 60 oak species in the U.S. Two oak groups, red and white, with the Black Oak a member of the red oak group. Acorns of the red oak group mature in two seasons, while white oak group acorns mature in one season. Has heavy fruit crops only infrequently. Nuts are bitter due to tannic acid (tannin). Bark also contains tannin, which was used in tanning animal skins. New leaves unfurling in spring are crimson before turning silvery, then dark green. Highly susceptible to oak wilt disease.

bark

flower

fruit

Red Oak
Quercus rubra

Family: Beech (Fagaceae)

Height: 50–70' (15–21 m)

Tree: single straight trunk, broad round crown

Leaf: lobed, 4–9" (10–22.5 cm) long, alternately attached, 7–11 lobes, each lobe ending in several pointed tips (bristle-tipped), with sinuses cutting only halfway to midrib, tufts of hair on veins underneath, dull yellow green

Bark: dark gray color and smooth texture when young, becoming light gray and deeply furrowed with flat narrow ridges with age

Flower: green catkin, 1–4" (2.5–10 cm) long, composed of many tiny flowers, ⅛" (.3 cm) wide

Fruit: green acorn, turning brown when mature, ½–1" (1–2.5 cm) long, on a short stalk, cap covering the upper quarter of nut

Fall Color: red to brown

Origin/Age: native; 100–150 years

Habitat: moist soils, also does well in dry soils, sun

Range: western half of the Carolinas

Stan's Notes: This is a member of the red oak group. The wood is reddish brown, giving the species name *rubra*, meaning "red," as well as the common name, Red. Differentiated from other red oaks by the leaf sinuses in between lobes cutting only halfway to the midrib. The pointed leaves and acorns that mature in two seasons distinguish it from the white oak group, which has rounded leaves and acorns that mature in one season. Its bitter nuts are not popular with wildlife. Succumbs to oak wilt, dying a few weeks after infection. Red Oak wood is used in flooring, furniture and many other products.

bark

fruit

Southern Red Oak
Quercus falcata

Family: Beech (Fagaceae)

Height: 60–80' (18–24.5 m)

Tree: medium to large tree with a single straight trunk, thick branches, rusty red twigs and an open well-rounded crown

Leaf: lobed, 5–9" (12.5–22.5 cm) in length, alternately attached, 3–5 long narrow lobes, each ending in 1–3 pointed tips (bristle-tipped), deep sinuses, shiny green above, lighter below with rust or gray hairs

Bark: dark gray to brown, many broad ridges and plates

Fruit: green acorn, turning brown when mature, edible, oblong or round, ½–¾" (1–2 cm) long, on a short stalk, red brown cap covering the upper third of nut, maturing in 2 seasons

Fall Color: brown

Origin/Age: native; 100–150 years

Habitat: dry sandy soils, upland in mixed forests, sun to partial shade

Range: throughout

Stan's Notes: As its common name implies, this tree grows mainly in the southern states, from Florida north to southern New York and west to Oklahoma. A fast-growing species that provides valuable shade. Leaves can be highly variable. Only some have three irregular lobes, but all always have pointed tips. Lumber is used for flooring and furniture. Like several other tree species, sometimes called Spanish Oak. Also known as Swamp Red Oak.

bark

fruit

Overcup Oak
Quercus lyrata

Family: Beech (Fagaceae)

Height: 40–60' (12–18 m)

Tree: medium tree, single straight trunk with numerous spreading branches, many lower branches often drooping downward, broad round crown

Leaf: lobed, 5–10" (12.5–25 cm) in length, alternately attached, 5–9 rounded lobes, toothless margin, dark green above, paler below and often with scattered whitish hairs

Bark: light gray to brown, thick with scaly furrows

Fruit: green acorn, turning brown when mature, edible, ½–1" (1–2.5 cm) long, thin scaly cap nearly covering the nut

Fall Color: yellow or red, turning brown

Origin/Age: native; 150–200 years

Habitat: poor soils, wet clay, floodplains, along swamps and other wet areas, sun or partial shade

Range: eastern two-thirds of the Carolinas

Stan's Notes: Also known as Swamp Post Oak or Swamp White Oak (not the Swamp White Oak on pg. 239) due to its preferred habitat of wet soils. Very tolerant of flooding and can survive when roots are covered with standing water. A slow-growing, long-lived tree that may take up to 30 years before producing acorns. Nuts are edible and eaten by wildlife. Common name "Overcup" refers to the acorn cap, which nearly covers the nut. Latin species name *lyrata* means "lyre-shaped" and refers to the shape of the leaf, resembling the lyre, a musical instrument.

bark

fruit

Cherrybark Oak
Quercus pagoda

Family: Beech (Fagaceae)

Height: 70–130' (21–40 m)

Tree: large tree, single trunk, dense large broad crown up to 100' (30.5 m) wide

Leaf: lobed, 4–7" (10–18 cm) long, alternately attached, 5 to 11 deep lobes with single tooth point, thick, bright shiny green above, and densely white hairs below

Bark: dark brown to reddish brown, thick, shallow furrows with flat scales and ridges

Fruit: green acorn, turning brown at maturity, edible, ovate, ½–1" (1–2.5 cm) long, cap covering upper third of nut, maturing in 1 season

Fall Color: green to brown

Origin/Age: native; 150–225 years

Habitat: moist or poorly drained bottomlands or floodplains, sun

Range: throughout the Carolinas, planted throughout in parks and yards

Stan's Notes: Can be a large and impressive tree and is prized for its straight hard wood. Was once considered a subspecies of the Southern Red Oak (pg. 249), but it is now considered its own species. Grows in low moist areas, which differentiates it from Southern Red Oak. Among the largest of the red oaks in the southern states. One of the hardiest and fastest growing of all oak species, making it a good tree to be planted in parks and yards. The species name *pagoda* is in reference to the arrangement of the leaves in distinct tiers, reminiscent of the shape of a pagoda. The common name "Cherrybark" refers to its bark, which looks similar to that of a cherry tree.

fruit

bark

flower

Boxelder
Acer negundo

COMPOUND
OPPOSITE

Family: Maple (Aceraceae)

Height: 30–50' (9–15 m)

Tree: medium-sized tree, frequently with a divided and crooked trunk, broad irregular crown

Leaf: compound, 4–9" (10–22.5 cm) in length, oppositely attached, made of 3–5 leaflets, each leaflet 2–4" (5–10 cm) in length, often 3-lobed, irregular-toothed margin, pale green

Bark: light gray to tan, becoming deeply furrowed with wavy ridges

Flower: tiny reddish flower, ¼" (.6 cm) wide, growing on a 1–3" (2.5–7.5 cm) long stalk

Fruit: pair of green winged seeds (samara), turning to brown, 1–2" (2.5–5 cm) long

Fall Color: yellow

Origin/Age: native; 50–60 years

Habitat: wet, along streams, lakes and flooded areas, sun

Range: throughout

Stan's Notes: Unique species among native maple trees because its leaves are compound. A member of the Maple family with all the virtues, but none of the respect. Frequently thought of as a trash tree, but it produces large amounts of seeds that stay on the tree during winter, making a valuable food source for wildlife. If the tree is tapped in spring, it will yield a sap that can be boiled into maple syrup. Since its sugar content is lower than that of the other maples, it takes more sap to make a comparable syrup. These trees are often covered with Boxelder Bugs, harmless beetles whose larvae eat the leaves but cause little damage. Also called Manitoba Maple or Ash-leaved Maple.

bark

fruit

American Bladdernut

Staphylea trifolia

Family: Bladdernut (Staphyleaceae)

Height: 20–25' (6–7.5 m)

Tree: small tree, multiple thin trunks, open crown

Leaf: compound, 6–9" (15–22.5 cm) long, oppositely attached, made of 3–5 oval leaflets, each leaflet 1–3" (2.5–7.5 cm) in length, with 2 pointed, nearly stalkless side leaflets and 1 long-stalked center, fine-toothed margin, dark green above and paler green below

Bark: gray, smooth, often becoming scaly and cracked with age

Fruit: 3-lobed green capsule, turning brown at maturity, 1–2" (2.5–5 cm) long, hanging down, opening at pointed end to release shiny brown round seeds

Fall Color: yellow, turning brown

Origin/Age: native; 30–50 years

Habitat: moist soils, understory of deciduous forests, shade

Range: scattered locations throughout the Carolinas

Stan's Notes: Often overlooked because it grows in the understory of deciduous forests. Species name *trifolia* refers to the three leaflets (tri-folia) of its compound leaf. Common name refers to its unique inflated green-to-brown bladders. The bladders, which are usually seen in summer and autumn, help to identify this tree. About 50 species of trees in this family with only two native to North America.

bark

flower

fruit

Carolina Ash
Fraxinus caroliniana

Family: Olive (Oleaceae)

Height: 20–40' (6–12 m)

Tree: single or multiple trunks, often leaning, enlarged base (buttress), narrow rounded crown

Leaf: compound, 5–12" (12.5–30 cm) long, oppositely attached, composed of 3–7 leaflets, each leaflet 2–4" (5–10 cm) long, coarse-toothed margin, green above, paler green to whitish and often slightly hairy below, on a thin long leaflet stalk (petiolule)

Bark: light gray, thin and scaly when young, becoming more scaly with age

Flower: green flower, ⅛" (.3 cm) wide, in loose clusters

Fruit: small green winged (sometimes 3-winged) seed (samara), turning yellow to brown at maturity, 1¼–2" (3–5 cm) long, large broad wing, in clusters

Fall Color: yellow

Origin/Age: native; 40–70 years

Habitat: wet soils, along streams, rivers and swamps, shade to partial sun

Range: eastern half of the Carolinas

Stan's Notes: A small to medium tree of wet habitats and along the coast. Ranges as far west as eastern Texas and farther southeast than any other *Fraxinus* tree, extending well into southern Florida. Also called Water or Swamp Ash for its water-loving habitat or Florida Ash. Male and female flowers are found on separate trees (dioecious), resulting in only female trees bearing seeds each season. Large broad winged seeds help to identify this species. One of the smallest of ash species in the eastern U.S., but has some of the largest winged seeds. Some say this is a commercially unimportant tree.

fruit

bark

White Ash
Fraxinus americana

Family: Olive (Oleaceae)

Height: 40–60' (12–18 m)

Tree: medium-sized tree with single straight trunk and narrow, open round crown

Leaf: compound, 8–12" (20–30 cm) in length, oppositely attached, composed of 7 (occasionally 5–9) oval leaflets, each leaflet 3–5" (7.5–12.5 cm) long, with few teeth or toothless, dark green above, distinctly whiter in color below, on a leaflet stalk (petiolule), ¼–½" (.6–1 cm) long

Bark: greenish gray with many furrows and interlacing diamond-shaped ridges

Fruit: green winged seed (samara), turning brown when mature, 1–2" (2.5–5 cm) long, notched or rounded wing tip, remaining on tree into winter

Fall Color: bronze purple

Origin/Age: native; 150–200 years

Habitat: well-drained soils, upland sites, sun

Range: western half of the Carolinas

Stan's Notes: Very similar to the Green Ash (pg. 265), but tends to grow in sunny, dry, well-drained upland sites. It is by far the most abundant of all 16 ash tree species in the U.S. A fast-growing tree, able to reach a height of up to 10 feet (3 m) in just under 5 years. Produces seeds annually and unusually large masses of seeds every 2–5 years. Young sprouts emerge from stumps or after fire damage. Common name "White" refers to the pale underside of leaves. The straight narrow-grained wood is used to make baseball bats, snowshoes and hockey sticks.

bark

fruit

Pumpkin Ash
Fraxinus profunda

Family: Olive (Oleaceae)

Height: 60–80' (18–24.5 m)

Tree: medium to large tree, single slender trunk with a flared base (buttress), narrow crown

Leaf: compound, 8–16" (20–40 cm) long, oppositely attached, composed of 7–9 leaflets, each leaflet 3–7" (7.5–18 cm) long, toothless margin, dark green above, yellowish with soft hairs below

Bark: gray with forking furrows, often forming diamond-shaped patterns

Fruit: green winged seed (samara), turning brown when mature, 2–3" (5–7.5 cm) long, hanging in clusters

Fall Color: yellow

Origin/Age: native; 75–100 years

Habitat: wet soils, swamps, wet woodlands, river valleys, sun

Range: eastern third of the Carolinas

Stan's Notes: An uncommon tree found along the coastal region of the Carolinas. Also seen in other parts of the U.S., such as scattered along Mississippi River valley. Its unique flared base resembles the base of the Bald Cypress (pg. 3), which grows in similar habitats. Common name "Pumpkin" refers to the enlarged, pumpkin-shaped base. Produces the largest seeds of all the native ash trees. Starts producing seeds at 10 years of age or older. Seeds are eaten by wildlife and remain on the tree well into winter. Sometimes called Red Ash, a common name shared by several tree species.

bark

fruit

Green Ash
Fraxinus pennsylvanica

Family: Olive (Oleaceae)

Height: 50–60' (15–18 m)

Tree: single straight trunk with ascending branches and irregular crown

Leaf: compound, 9–16" (22.5–40 cm) long, oppositely attached, made of 5–9 stalked leaflets, each leaflet 1–2" (2.5–5 cm) long, lacking teeth or with a very fine-toothed margin, on a very short leaflet stalk (petiolule), ⅛" (.3 cm) long

Bark: brown with deep furrows and narrow interlacing ridges, often appearing diamond-shaped

Fruit: green winged seed (samara), turning brown when mature, 1–2" (2.5–5 cm) in length, mostly round-ended, sometimes notched, in clusters, frequently remaining on tree into winter

Fall Color: yellow

Origin/Age: native; 75–100 years

Habitat: wet soils, along streams, lowland forests, shade

Range: throughout, planted in parks and yards

Stan's Notes: Found in most of the eastern U.S. Also known as Red Ash because it was once thought that Green Ash and Red Ash trees were separate species. These are now considered one species. Not as water tolerant as the Pumpkin Ash (pg. 263), but able to survive with its roots under water for several weeks early in spring. Often has a large unattractive growth (insect gall) at the ends of small branches that persists on the tree throughout the year. The strong white wood is used for baseball bats, skis and snowshoes.

bark

fruit

Common Hoptree
Ptelea trifoliata

Family: Rue (Rutaceae)

Height: 20–25' (6–7.5 m)

Tree: small tree, single straight trunk, branching low to the ground, full round crown

Leaf: compound, 4–7" (10–18 cm) in length, alternately attached, composed of 3 leaflets, each leaflet 2–4" (5–10 cm) long, wider in middle with pointed tip, smooth toothless margin, shiny dark green above, much lighter below with many tiny translucent dots that can be seen when held up to the light, lacking a leaflet stalk (sessile), attaching directly to the central stalk (rachis), which is 3" (7.5 cm) long

Bark: reddish brown, smooth

Fruit: wafer-like flat green disk (samara), turning yellow-brown and papery, up to 1" (2.5 cm) wide, wavy margin, remaining on tree well into winter

Fall Color: yellow

Origin/Age: native; 30–50 years

Habitat: well-drained dry soils, along forest edges, open woodlands, sun to partial shade

Range: throughout

Stan's Notes: A member of the Rue family (Citrus), which explains why its leaves have a strong citrus scent when crushed. Leaflets are often many different sizes. Seeds were used at one time in brewing beer as a substitute for hops, hence the common name. Like many trees with aromatic leaves and bark, it has been used for many ailments for its medicinal properties. Fruit matures late in summer. An easy tree to identify without leaves because its mature yellow-brown fruit remains on the tree. Also called Stinking-ash or Wafer-ash.

bark

flower

fruit

Yellowwood
Cladrastis kentukea

Family: Pea or Bean (Fabaceae)

Height: 20–40' (6–12 m)

Tree: small to medium tree with a single straight trunk, ascending branches, broad round crown

Leaf: compound, 8–12" (20–30 cm) long, alternately attached, composed of 5–11 oval-shaped leaflets, each leaflet 2–4" (5–10 cm) long, also alternately attached, smooth margin, yellowish green above, paler below, nearly stalkless

Bark: gray bark, usually smooth and appearing thin

Flower: many 5-petaled white flowers with yellow centers, each 1–1¼" (2.5–3 cm) long, in clusters, drooping on a long stalk, fragrant

Fruit: green pod, 3–4" (7.5–10 cm) long, turning brown when mature, long, flat and narrow, hanging in clusters, containing 2–6 seeds

Fall Color: yellow to gold to orange

Origin/Age: native; 50–100 years

Habitat: moist soils, moist valleys, along streams and other wet places, sun

Range: western quarter of North Carolina

Stan's Notes: A slow-growing tree with unusual compound leaves. While most trees with compound leaves have oppositely attached leaflets, Yellowwood leaflets are alternately attached. Freshly cut wood is yellow, and twigs that are crushed smell like dried beans. Of the eight known trees in the genus *Cladrastis*, the Yellowwood is the only one native to the U.S. The others occur in China and Japan. Sometimes called Kentucky Yellowwood.

thorn

bark

flower

fruit

Black Locust
Robinia pseudoacacia

Family: Pea or Bean (Fabaceae)

Height: 30–50' (9–15 m)

Tree: medium-sized tree, often crooked trunk, upright spreading branches, open irregular crown

Leaf: compound, 7–14" (18–36 cm) in length, alternately attached, composed of 7–19 oval to round leaflets, each leaflet 1–2" (2.5–5 cm) in length, lacks teeth, yellowish green

Bark: dark brown color and smooth texture, becoming furrowed and scaly with age, opposite pairs of stout thorns (see inset), especially on young trees

Flower: pea-like white flower with yellow center, ½–1" (1–2.5 cm) wide, in hanging clusters, 2–4" (5–10 cm) long, appearing soon after leaves develop, fragrant

Fruit: green pod, turning brown when mature, flat, 2–4" (5–10 cm) long, containing 4–8 seeds

Fall Color: yellow

Origin/Age: native; 75–100 years

Habitat: adapts to almost any type of soil, moist woods, shade intolerant

Range: western quarter of the Carolinas, planted throughout along roads, in parks, around homes

Stan's Notes: Fifteen species of locust trees and shrubs, all native to North America. Wood is so strong that in the 1800s the British credited success of the U.S. naval fleet in the War of 1812 to Black Locust lumber, used to build ships. Roots combine with bacteria, fixing atmospheric nitrogen into the soil. Spreads rapidly by root suckering. Branches and twigs have stout thorns in pairs at bases of leafstalks. Susceptible to Locust Borer beetles, which bore into trunks.

bark

flower

fruit

Tree-of-heaven
Ailanthus altissima

Family: Quassia (Simaroubaceae)

Height: 50–70' (15–21 m)

Tree: medium tree, single or multiple crooked trunks, many stout branches, open round crown

Leaf: compound, 12–24" (30–60 cm) long, alternately attached, composed of 13–25 (sometimes more) lance-shaped leaflets, each 3–5" (7.5–12.5 cm) long, toothless except for 2–5 teeth near the base, each tooth accompanied by a tiny gland on underside of leaflet, light green above, paler below

Bark: light brown, smooth, becoming rough with age

Flower: 5-petaled yellowish green flower, ¼" (.6 cm) wide, in large conical clusters, 6–11" (15–28 cm) tall, at the tip of branch

Fruit: green winged seed, turning red at maturity in late summer, flat, 1¼–1½" (3–4 cm) long

Fall Color: yellow

Origin/Age: non-native; 50–75 years

Habitat: wide variety of soils, abandoned fields, old farms

Range: planted in parks, yards and along streets

Stan's Notes: A fast-growing tree introduced from northern China around 1874. Planted widely as an ornamental due to its hardiness and rapid growth, 5–8 feet (1.5–2.4 m) per year. A very difficult tree to eradicate once established. Male flowers have an unpleasant odor. Flowers bloom after leaves are developed, unlike most native trees. Produces large clusters of winged seeds during late summer, which remain on the tree into winter. Survives well in cities. Presumably the species in Betty Smith's novel *A Tree Grows in Brooklyn*. Native to Asia and northern Australia with about ten *Ailanthus* species.

bark

flower

fruit

European Mountain-ash
Sorbus aucuparia

Family: Rose (Rosaceae)

Height: 15–25' (4.5–7.5 m)

Tree: single trunk, ascending branches, round crown

Leaf: compound, 4–8" (10–20 cm) in length, alternately attached, made of 9–17 oval leaflets, each leaflet 1–2" (2.5–5 cm) long, with fine-toothed margin, dull green above, whitish below, central stalk (rachis) often yellowish

Bark: shiny gray in color, smooth with many horizontal lines (lenticels)

Flower: greenish flower, ¼" (.6 cm) wide, in flat clusters, 3–5" (7.5–12.5 cm) wide

Fruit: orange to red berry-like fruit (pome), ¼" (.6 cm) diameter, in hanging clusters, 3–5" (7.5–12.5 cm) long, each containing 1–2 shiny black seeds

Fall Color: yellow

Origin/Age: non-native, introduced from Europe; 25–50 years

Habitat: dry soils, old fields, abandoned farms, sun

Range: planted in parks, yards and along roads

Stan's Notes: A member of the Rose family and not a type of ash tree, it is by far the most commonly planted type of mountain-ash tree. Nearly identical to American Mountain-ash (pg. 277), except for the yellowish central stalk. Often a favorite tree of Yellow-bellied Sapsuckers. Spread by birds passing seeds through their digestive tracts unharmed. Latin species name *aucuparia* comes from *avis* and *capere*, meaning "to catch birds," suggesting the fruit was used to bait bird traps. The berry-like fruit provides a good source of food for birds and other wildlife. Containing high amounts of vitamin C, it was once used to cure scurvy. Also called Rowan-tree.

bark

flower

fruit

American Mountain-ash
Sorbus americana

Family: Rose (Rosaceae)

Height: 15–30' (4.5–9 m)

Tree: small tree, often shrub-like with multiple trunks, open round crown

Leaf: compound, 6–9" (15–22.5 cm) in length, alternately attached, with 11–17 lance-shaped leaflets, each leaflet 2–4" (5–10 cm) long, fine sharp teeth, pale green, central stalk (rachis) often reddish

Bark: light gray color, many elongated horizontal lines (lenticels), smooth, becoming very scaly with age

Flower: white-to-cream flower, ¼" (.6 cm) wide, in flat clusters, 3–5" (7.5–12.5 cm) wide

Fruit: bright orange or red berry-like fruit (pome), ¼" (.6 cm) diameter, in hanging clusters, 3–5" (7.5–12.5 cm) wide

Fall Color: yellow

Origin/Age: native; 25–50 years

Habitat: cool moist sites, wetland and forest edges, rocky hillsides, shade

Range: western quarter of the Carolinas

Stan's Notes: This slow-growing ornamental tree is widely planted in landscapes for its showy flowers and resulting brightly colored fruit. A favorite forage of deer. Often a favorite tree of Yellow-bellied Sapsuckers, which drill rows of horizontal holes and lap up the sap. Birds, especially Cedar Waxwings and Ruffed Grouse, consume the berry-like fruit. Cultivated varieties are often planted to attract birds. A sun-intolerant tree, susceptible to fire blight disease and sunscald. About 75 species of mountain-ash worldwide.

thorn

bark

fruit

Common Prickly-ash
Zanthoxylum americanum

Family: Rue (Rutaceae)

Height: 5–15' (1.5–4.5 m)

Tree: small tree, single or multiple trunks, round crown

Leaf: compound, 5–10" (12.5–25 cm) long, alternately attached, made up of 5–11 oval leaflets, each leaflet 1–2" (2.5–5 cm) in length, lacking teeth, citrus scent when crushed, dull green

Bark: gray, smooth with dark gray marks (lenticels) and white blotches, stout sharp thorns on branches

Fruit: green berry-like fruit (pome), turning bright red when mature, ¼" (.6 cm) diameter, in clusters, splitting open in fall and releasing the seed, strong orange or lemon-like citrus scent when crushed

Fall Color: yellow

Origin/Age: native; 25–30 years

Habitat: wide variety of soils, along forest edges, sun to partial shade

Range: scattered in isolated locations throughout the Carolinas

Stan's Notes: One of two members of the Rue (sometimes referred to as Citrus) family in the Carolinas. This is a small tree with stout sharp thorns covering its branches. The leaves and especially the berry-like fruit contain zanthoxylin, a citrus-smelling oil. Fruit and inner bark cause numbness in the mouth and have been used for treatment of toothaches, hence its other common name, Toothache Tree. The Greek genus name *Zanthoxylum* means "yellow wood" and describes the wood color. It reproduces from underground roots and forms thick stands along forest edges. The fruit is highly fragrant when it is crushed, smelling like a combination of oranges, lemons and limes.

bark

fruit

Sand Hickory
Carya pallida

Family: Walnut (Juglandaceae)

Height: 30–50' (9–15 m)

Tree: small tree with a single straight trunk, dense erect crown, lower branches drooping

Leaf: compound, 8–15" (20–38 cm) long, alternately attached, made of 5–9 oval leaflets, each leaflet 3–6" (7.5–15 cm) long, pointed at the tip, narrower at the base, wider in the middle, fine toothed, glossy green above, paler and silvery hairy below, especially the main vein, lacking a leaflet stalk (sessile), leaf buds have rusty scales and hairs.

Bark: grayish, thick and smooth when young, becoming scaly and with furrows forming small diamond shapes with age

Fruit: green pear-shaped fruit covered with yellow-to-brown hairs, turning brown when mature, 1–1½" (2.5–4 cm) wide, 4-sided thin brown shell splits open, inner nutmeat (kernel) edible

Fall Color: yellow

Origin/Age: native; 200–400 years

Habitat: dry and sandy soils on plains, rocky valleys in lower elevations, sun to partial shade

Range: throughout

Stan's Notes: Common throughout both states. Male and female flowers are found on the same tree (monoecious), but they emerge at different times to stop self-pollination. Sometimes called Pale Hickory or Pignut Hickory. The species name *pallida* mean "pale" and refers to the underside of the leaflets. Like many trees, it produces large nut crops every couple of years, providing a much-needed food source for wildlife.

immature
fruit

bark

fruit

Bitternut Hickory
Carya cordiformis

Family: Walnut (Juglandaceae)

Height: 50–100' (15–30.5 m)

Tree: large tree, sturdy straight trunk, slender upright branches, open round crown

Leaf: compound, 6–10" (15–25 cm) in length, alternately attached, made up of 7–11 narrow leaflets, each leaflet 3–6" (7.5–15 cm) long, with pointed tip and fine-toothed margin, shiny green above, paler in color below, lacks a leaflet stalk (sessile), attaching directly to the central stalk (rachis)

Bark: gray in color with irregular vertical cracks, scaly in appearance but never loose scales

Fruit: nut, too bitter to be edible, round, ¾–1½" (2–4 cm) diameter, with pointed end, 4 ridges extending to point, yellowish hairs covering outer husk

Fall Color: golden yellow

Origin/Age: native; 100–150 years

Habitat: moist soils, lowlands, shade intolerant

Range: throughout

Stan's Notes: The most extensive and northerly of hickories, it is slow growing and shade intolerant. Its large, distinctive yellow buds are diagnostic before the leaves emerge. The wood is used to smoke meat and produces the best flavor of all hickories. Meat of the nuts is very bitter and unpalatable to humans and much wildlife, hence the common name. Oil extracted from the nuts was used for lamp fuel. Sometimes called Bitter Pecan because it is closely related to the familiar pecan. Also called Swamp Hickory due to its preference for wet or loamy soils. Hickories are found naturally in eastern North America and Asia. About 15 species are native to North America.

fruit

bark

Red Hickory
Carya glabra

Family: Walnut (Juglandaceae)

Height: 60–80' (18–24.5 m)

Tree: medium to large tree, single straight trunk, bottom quarter often branch-free, short crooked branches, tips often pointing down, narrow round crown

Leaf: compound, 6–10" (15–25 cm) in length, alternately attached, composed of 5 (rarely 7) lance-shaped leaflets, each leaflet 3–6" (7.5–15 cm) long, wider in middle, fine-toothed margin, midrib covered with hair, yellowish green above and paler below, terminal and first pair of leaflets larger than leaflets closest to stem, nearly stalkless

Bark: gray, becoming very shaggy with age, often peeling into long, thin, loosely attached strips

Fruit: pear-shaped to round green nuts, turning brown when mature, 1–2" (2.5–5 cm) diameter, in small clusters, thin shell splitting open into 4 sections, inedible nut

Fall Color: yellow

Origin/Age: native; 150–200 years

Habitat: well-drained dry soils, hillsides, dry ridges, sun

Range: throughout

Stan's Notes: One of the most common hickories in the eastern U.S. Also called Pignut Hickory because the nuts were considered fit only for hogs. Flavor is actually highly variable—some nuts are sweet, others are bitter. Was called Broom Hickory because broom handles were made from saplings. Wood was once used in wagon wheels. Usually in mixed stands of deciduous trees in upland sites, unlike Shellbark Hickory (pg. 293), which grows in moist to wet sites.

bark

fruit

twig pith

Shagbark Hickory
Carya ovata

COMPOUND ALTERNATE

Family: Walnut (Juglandaceae)

Height: 40–60' (12–18 m)

Tree: medium-sized tree with single straight trunk and tall, narrow irregular crown

Leaf: compound, 8–14" (20–36 cm) in length, alternately attached, with 5 (rarely 7) pointed leaflets, each leaflet 3–4" (7.5–10 cm) long, widest at the middle, upper 3 leaflets larger than lower 2, fine-toothed margin, yellowish green, lacks leaflet stalk (sessile), attaching directly to central stalk (rachis)

Bark: gray in color, long smooth vertical strips curling at each end, giving it a shaggy appearance

Fruit: green nut, turning brown at maturity, inner kernel sweet, edible, round to ovate, 1–1½" (2.5–4 cm) in diameter, single or in pairs, thick 4-ribbed husk

Fall Color: yellow

Origin/Age: native; 150–200 years

Habitat: rich moist soils, hillsides, slopes, bottomlands, sun

Range: western quarter of the Carolinas

Stan's Notes: Also called Upland Hickory. Often found on hillsides that have rich moist soils, growing branch-free for three-quarters of its height. Its common name comes from the large scaly or "shaggy" bark. Also known as Shell-bark or Seal-bark Hickory. Hickories are divided into two groups: true hickories, which include Shagbark, and pecan hickories, which include Bitternut Hickory (pg. 283). Shagbark nuts are eaten by wildlife and people. Its extremely hard wood is used to make tool handles, skis and wagon wheels. Unlike the twigs of walnut trees, which have a light brown pith, twigs of this species have a white pith (see inset).

287

bark

immature fruit

fruit

Mockernut Hickory
Carya tomentosa

Family: Walnut (Juglandaceae)

Height: 40–80' (12–24.5 m)

Tree: medium to large tree, usually has a straight trunk, branchless to halfway up, narrow round crown

Leaf: compound, 8–20" (20–50 cm) in length, alternately attached, made of 7–9 leaflets, each leaflet 2–8" (5–20 cm) in length, elliptical, pointed at tip, round at base, wider middle, fine-toothed, shiny dark green above, paler and hairy below, leaflet nearly stalkless

Bark: gray to light brown with narrow forked ridges

Fruit: thick-shelled green nut, 1½–2" (4–5 cm) diameter, turning brown when mature, inner kernel edible, tan to light brown, ¾–1" (2–2.5 cm) wide, 4-sided

Fall Color: yellow

Origin/Age: native; 300–500 years

Habitat: moist upland sites, frequently with oaks and other hickories on ridges and hillsides, sun

Range: throughout

Stan's Notes: A straight-growing hickory, common in the eastern half of the U.S. Wood has been valued for its strength for furniture; also used for smoking meat, such as ham. Species name comes from the Latin word *tomentum*, meaning "covered with dense short hairs," referring to the underside of leaves and helping identify the species. Also called White Hickory due to the light color of the wood. The common name "Mockernut" comes from the large thick-shelled fruit with very small kernels of meat inside. Its nuts are an important wildlife food; many birds and animals eat or store them for winter. Produces nuts after 20 years, but the prime nut-bearing age is from 50 to 150 years old. Stout, hairy twigs, often reddish brown.

bark

fruit

Nutmeg Hickory
Carya myristiciformis

Family: Walnut (Juglandaceae)

Height: 70–80' (21–24 m)

Tree: medium tree with a single straight trunk, narrow open crown

Leaf: compound, 6–14" (15–36 cm) long, alternately attached, made of 5–9 oval leaflets, each leaflet 2–5" (5–13 cm) long, pointed at the tip, narrower at the base, wider in the middle, coarsely toothed, dark green above, paler and sometimes hairy below, especially the main vein, lacking a leaflet stalk (sessile)

Bark: reddish brown, thick and smooth when young, becoming scaly with age

Fruit: green fruit covered with yellow-to-brown hairs, turning brown when mature, 1–1½" (2.5–4 cm) wide, 4-sided thin shell splits open, inner nutmeat (kernel) edible

Fall Color: bronze

Origin/Age: native; 200–400 years

Habitat: moist river bottoms, sun to partial shade

Range: isolated to wet or moist areas in coastal and central South Carolina

Stan's Notes: The rarest *Carya* species, scattered in South Carolina in moist low-lying areas. Not much is known about this species. Species name *myristiciformis* refers to nutmeg, as the nut appears similar to nutmeg in size and shape. Produces a large nut crop every 2–3 years, providing food for wildlife. Wild specimens are often misidentified. When cut for commercial use they are often referred to just as Hickory or Pecan. Has golden-brown twigs and bronze-colored scales on the underside of the leaves, twigs and leaf buds.

bark

fruit

Shellbark Hickory
Carya laciniosa

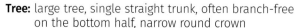

Family: Walnut (Juglandaceae)

Height: 70–90' (21–27.5 m)

Tree: large tree, single straight trunk, often branch-free on the bottom half, narrow round crown

Leaf: compound, 12–20" (30–50 cm) in length, alternately attached, composed of 7 (rarely 9) lance-shaped leaflets, each leaflet 2–8" (5–20 cm) in length, fine-toothed margin, shiny green above, paler below and covered with soft hair

Bark: gray, becoming rough and shaggy with age, often peeling into long, thin, loosely attached strips

Fruit: thick-shelled green fruit, turning dark brown at maturity, edible, round, 2–3" (5–7.5 cm) diameter, husk splits open into 4 sections, releasing a nearly round nut

Fall Color: yellow

Origin/Age: native; 150–200 years

Habitat: moist to wet soils, floodplains, sun to part shade

Range: scattered locations in western North Carolina, planted in parks and yards

Stan's Notes: The Shellbark's large leaves, extremely large fruit and orange twigs make it one of the easiest hickories to identify. Orange twigs are distinctive, but not always obvious. Similar scaly bark as Shagbark Hickory (pg. 287), but the Shellbark has more leaflets and larger fruit. The Latin species name *laciniosa* means "with folds" and refers to the characteristic shaggy bark. Also known as Big Shagbark Hickory or Kingnut, referring to the oversized fruit. Fruit is edible and eaten by wildlife. Central stalk (rachis) remains on the tree after the leaflets fall each autumn.

bark

immature fruit

fruit

Pecan
Carya illinoensis

Family: Walnut (Juglandaceae)

Height: 70–100' (21–30 m)

Tree: large tree with a single trunk and tall, broad round crown composed of long spreading branches

Leaf: compound, 12–20" (30–51 cm) long, alternately attached, composed of 11–17 slightly curved leaflets, each leaflet 2–7" (5–18 cm) long, with a pointed tip and fine saw-toothed margin, yellowish green above, paler below

Bark: light brown and smooth, turning gray and deeply furrowed into scaly ridges with age

Fruit: green fruit, turning brown at maturity, oblong and pointed, 1–2" (2.5–5 cm) long, in clusters of 3–7, thin husk splits along 4 ridges, releasing a hard-shelled nut with a sweet, edible nutmeat (kernel)

Fall Color: yellow

Origin/Age: non-native; 150–300 years

Habitat: moist soils, along river valleys and floodplains, sun to partial shade

Range: throughout both states, planted in parks and yards

Stan's Notes: One of the largest of hickories, sometimes growing higher than 100 feet (30 m). It is widespread in the Carolinas due to planting in parks and yards and plantations. Improved varieties that produce thin-shelled nuts are planted in large orchards on plantations, where millions of nuts are collected and processed annually. Often planted in yards for the nuts. Latin species name *illinoensis* means "from Illinois" and refers to the area where it was first described by early traders. Was an important food source for American Indians, who may have expanded its range by planting it as they relocated.

flower

bark

fruit

Poison Sumac

Toxicodendron vernix

Family: Cashew (Anacardiaceae)

Height: 5–20' (1.5–6 m)

Tree: small tree, single trunk, few horizontal branches, open irregular crown

Leaf: compound, 6–12" (15–30 cm) in length, alternately attached, composed of 7–13 lance-shaped leaflets, each leaflet 1½–3" (4–7.5 cm) long, lacking teeth, smooth to touch, dark green above, pale white in color below, leaflet stalk (petiolule) and central stalk (rachis) often reddish

Bark: light gray, smooth

Flower: green flower, ¼" (.6 cm) wide, in clusters, 2–4" (5–10 cm) wide, on open branches

Fruit: green-to-glossy-white berry-like fruit (drupe), ¼" (.6 cm) diameter, remaining on tree into winter

Fall Color: yellow to red

Origin/Age: native; 50–75 years

Habitat: wet soils, bogs, sun

Range: scattered throughout the Carolinas

Stan's Notes: A rare tree found only in open swamps and bogs. Few if any encounter this tree due to its remote wet habitat and the rarity of the species. The oils of Poison Sumac are toxic, causing severe skin rash. If burned, the smoke can cause severe breathing difficulties, and irritated eyes and skin. Closely related to other sumacs in the Carolinas (pgs. 299 and 301) and to Poison Ivy.

flower

bark

fruit

Smooth Sumac
Rhus glabra

Family: Cashew (Anacardiaceae)

Height: 10–20' (3–6 m)

Tree: single or multiple trunks, closed flat-topped crown

Leaf: compound, 12–24" (30–60 cm) in length, alternately attached, with 11–31 leaflets, each leaflet 2–4" (5–10 cm) long, toothed margin, dark green above, some red hairs below, lacking a leaflet stalk (sessile), attaching directly to central stalk (rachis)

Bark: brown, smooth, rarely any furrows or scales

Flower: green flower, ¼" (.6 cm) diameter, in open wide upright clusters, 4–8" (10–20 cm) tall

Fruit: red berry-like fruit (drupe), ⅛" (.3 cm) diameter, in cone-shaped clusters, 4–8" (10–20 cm) long

Fall Color: red

Origin/Age: native; 25–50 years

Habitat: dry or poor soils, forest edges, sun

Range: throughout

Stan's Notes: One of the first trees to turn colors in fall. Over 100 species of sumac, most occurring in southern Africa. Closely related to the Staghorn Sumac (pg. 301), which has hairy central stalks and leaves. While Smooth Sumac is not as common as Staghorn, they hybridize where occurring together. Fast growing, reproducing by underground roots that send up new trunks. Often forms a dense stand. Once established, it is often hard to eradicate. Has been planted to stabilize slopes from erosion. Male and female flowers are on separate trees (dioecious), so not all sumacs produce the attractive clusters of red fruit. Animals and birds eat the berry-like fruit. Ripe sumac fruit is used to make a lemonade-like drink.

flower

bark

fruit

Staghorn Sumac
Rhus typhina

Family: Cashew (Anacardiaceae)

Height: 10–20' (3–6 m)

Tree: single or multiple trunks, closed flat-topped crown

Leaf: compound, 12–24" (30–60 cm) in length, alternately attached, composed of 11–31 leaflets, each leaflet 2–4" (5–10 cm) long, with toothed margin, dark green above, red hairs below, lacking a leaflet stalk (sessile), attaching directly to the central stalk (rachis), which is often hairy and reddish

Bark: brown, smooth, rarely any furrows or scales

Flower: green flower, ¼" (.6 cm) diameter, in tight cone-shaped clusters, 4–8" (10–20 cm) long

Fruit: fuzzy red berry-like fruit (drupe), ⅛" (.3 cm) wide, in thin cone-shaped clusters, 4–8" (10–20 cm) long

Fall Color: red to maroon

Origin/Age: native; 25–50 years

Habitat: dry or poor soils, forest edges, sun

Range: scattered throughout the Carolinas, planted along roads, in parks and yards

Stan's Notes: One of the first trees to turn colors each autumn. Its fuzzy central stalks resemble the velvety antlers of a deer, hence the common name. Closely related to Smooth Sumac (pg. 299), which lacks hairy leaves and central stalks. Reproduces by underground roots that send up new trunks. Fast growing, often forming a dense stand that extends up to several hundred feet in each direction. Often planted along highways for its rapid growth, thus stabilizing the soil quickly. Animals and birds eat the red berry-like fruit. "Sumac-ade" can be made from ripe sumac fruit.

twig pith

bark

flower

fruit

Black Walnut
Juglans nigra

COMPOUND
ALTERNATE

Family: Walnut (Juglandaceae)

Height: 50–75' (15–23 m)

Tree: straight trunk, open round crown

Leaf: compound, 12–24" (30–60 cm) in length, alternately attached, with 15–23 stalkless leaflets (sessile), each leaflet 3–4" (7.5–10 cm) long, with pointed tip, last (terminal) leaflet often smaller or absent, middle leaflets larger than on either end, fine-toothed margin, yellowish green and smooth above, slightly lighter and hairy below

Bark: brown to black, becoming darker with age, deep pits and flat scaly ridges

Flower: catkin, 2–4" (5–10 cm) long, composed of many tiny green flowers, ¼" (.6 cm) wide

Fruit: fleshy green fruit, round, 1–2" (2.5–5 cm) wide, in clusters, aromatic green husk surrounding a hard dark nut that matures in autumn, nutmeat sweet and edible

Fall Color: yellowish green

Origin/Age: native; 150–175 years

Habitat: well-drained rich soils, shade intolerant

Range: scattered throughout, planted in parks and yards

Stan's Notes: One of six species of walnut native to North America. Valued for its wood, which doesn't shrink or warp and is used to build furniture and cabinets. An important food source for wildlife. Fruit husks contain a substance that stains skin and were used by pioneers to dye clothing light brown. Twigs have a light brown chambered pith (see inset), unlike dark brown pith of Butternut (pg. 305). Fallen leaves and roots produce juglone, a natural herbicide.

immature
fruit

bark

fruit

twig pith

Butternut
Juglans cinerea

Family: Walnut (Juglandaceae)

Height: 40–60' (12–18 m)

Tree: medium-sized tree, usually a divided trunk, open broad and often flat crown

Leaf: compound, 15–25" (37.5–63 cm) long, alternately attached, made of 11–17 stalkless leaflets (sessile), each leaflet 2–4" (5–10 cm) in length, fine-toothed margin, last (terminal) leaflet usually present and same size as the lateral leaflets, and progressing smaller toward the leaf base, stout hairs covering each leaflet and the central stalk (rachis)

Bark: light gray with broad flat ridges

Flower: catkin, 1–2" (2.5–5 cm) long, composed of many tiny green flowers, ¼" (.6 cm) wide

Fruit: nut, edible, ovate, 2–3" (5–7.5 cm) long, in clusters, sticky green husk, turning brown

Fall Color: yellow

Origin/Age: native; 80–100 years

Habitat: wide variety of soils, often on slopes having well-drained rich soils, sun

Range: scattered in isolated locations throughout the Carolinas

Stan's Notes: A short-lived tree, also called White Walnut. Its very hard, strong wood is much sought by woodworkers. Twigs are stout with a dark brown chambered pith (see inset). The sap can be boiled to make syrup. Yellow dye can be extracted from the husks and used to color fabrics. Common name comes from its butter-like oil, which American Indians once extracted from the nuts. Butternut canker, caused by a fungus, has killed many of these trees.

thorn on trunk

bark

fruit

thorn

Water Locust
Gleditsia aquatica

Family: Pea or Bean (Fabaceae)

Height: 30–50' (9–15 m)

Tree: medium-sized tree with a short trunk divided low, broad flat-topped crown

Leaf: twice compound (sometimes compound), 4–8" (10–20 cm) long, alternately attached, composed of 15–30 oblong leaflets, each leaflet ½–1¼" (1–3 cm) long, wavy margin, stalkless (sessile), shiny dark green above, much duller below

Bark: brown to gray, thin and smooth, becoming scaly with age, many large branched thorns on trunk

Flower: 5-petaled green flower, ¼" (.6 cm) wide, in clusters, up to 4" (10 cm) long

Fruit: large pea-like green pod, flat, turning brown and papery at maturity, 1–2" (2.5–5 cm) long, in hanging clusters, containing 1 large flattened seed

Fall Color: yellow

Origin/Age: native; 100–125 years

Habitat: wet soils, along wetlands and rivers, partial shade to sun

Range: along the coast of South Carolina

Stan's Notes: A smaller version of the Honey Locust (pg. 309) and differentiated from it by the smaller-sized leaves and pulpless pods. Common name comes from its habit of growing in wet areas. Species name *aquatica* also refers to its water-loving nature. Not a favorite tree for planting in parks and yards because of its thorny branches and large clusters of thorns on its trunk (see insets). The wood is heavy, strong and hard and has been used for tool handles and fence posts.

bark

flower

fruit

Honey Locust
Gleditsia triacanthos

Family: Pea or Bean (Fabaceae)

Height: 40–60' (12–18 m)

Tree: single trunk is often divided low, open broad and sometimes flat-topped crown

Leaf: twice compound, 12–24" (30–60 cm) long, alternately attached, composed of 14–30 elliptical, feathery leaflets, each leaflet 1" (2.5 cm) in length, fine-toothed margin, dark green above and yellow green below

Bark: reddish brown covered with gray horizontal lines (lenticels), often cracking and peeling, frequently thorny on trunk and branches

Flower: small green catkin, 1–2" (2.5–5 cm) long

Fruit: large pea-like purplish brown pod, flat, twisted, 6–16" (15–40 cm) long, 12–14 oval seeds per pod

Fall Color: yellow

Origin/Age: non-native; 100–125 years

Habitat: moist or rich soils, sun

Range: planted in parks and yards and along roads

Stan's Notes: Also called Thorny Locust because it has large thorns on the trunk and branches and twigs are zigzagged with thorns at joints. Between seeds in seedpods is a sweet yellowish substance, hence "Honey" in the common name. Seedpods are large, obvious and eaten by wildlife. Should not be pruned in wet weather since it opens the tree to infection by *Nectria* canker. Thornless and seedless varieties are widely planted in parks and yards and along roads. Most varieties planted in landscaping lack thorns and fruit. Largest of the two species of *Gleditsia* native to North America.

bark

fruit

Kentucky Coffeetree
Gymnocladus dioicus

Family: Pea or Bean (Fabaceae)

Height: 40–60' (12–18 m)

Tree: single trunk, can be divided low, many crooked branches, open round crown

Leaf: twice compound, 12–36" (30–90 cm) long, alternately attached, made of many (up to 70) leaflets, each leaflet 2" (5 cm) long, lacks teeth, blue-green

Bark: brown and smooth when young, thin scales with edges curling out, breaking with age into plates

Flower: 5-petaled white flower, ¼–½" (.6–1 cm) diameter, on a single long stalk, in open clusters, 1–3" (2.5–7.5 cm) wide

Fruit: leathery green pod, turning reddish brown when mature, 4–10" (10–25 cm) in length, often covered with a whitish powder, containing 6–9 large seeds

Fall Color: yellow

Origin/Age: non-native; 50–75 years

Habitat: deep rich soils, sun

Range: planted in urban sites, farms, parks, along roads

Stan's Notes: The leaves of this species are among the last to appear in spring, first to turn in fall. Common name comes from its coffee-bean-like seeds in seedpods. The seedpods contain many dark seeds surrounded by a yellowish pulp that becomes soapy when wet. The bitter seeds are seldom eaten by wildlife and remain viable for several years. New trees sprout from roots of parent trees, often forming small colonies. The genus name *Gymnocladus* comes from the Greek for "naked branch," which is how the branches appear.

thorn

bark

flower

fruit

Devil's-walkingstick
Aralia spinosa

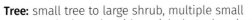

Family: Ginseng (Araliaceae)

Height: 20–30' (6–9 m)

Tree: small tree to large shrub, multiple small crooked trunks with upright branches, irregular to round crown

Leaf: twice compound, 13–36" (33–90 cm) long, alternately attached, composed of numerous leaflets, each leaflet 2–3½" (5–9 cm) long, with a pointed tip and toothed margin, dark green above, paler below with prickles on midrib

Bark: dark brown, thin fissures, scattered stout thorns

Flower: 5-petaled white-to-cream flower, ⅛" (.3 cm) wide, in large upright clusters, 8–16" (20–40 cm) long

Fruit: green berry, turning purplish when mature, ⅛–¼" (.3–.6 cm) wide, juicy and aromatic when ripe, in large clusters, each containing 3–5 seeds

Fall Color: yellow

Origin/Age: native; 25–30 years

Habitat: moist soils, near streams, shade tolerant

Range: throughout

Stan's Notes: There are more than 800 species of trees and shrubs in this family. These can be found all over the world, particularly in tropical areas. Also called Angelica Tree or Hercules-club, the latter common name due to the short thorns on the bark (see inset). Was once planted in Victorian gardens as an ornamental shrub. Has eye-catching large clusters of flowers and purplish mature fruit. Roots and fruit are extremely fragrant and were once used to cure many ailments, such as toothaches.

bark

flower

fruit

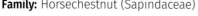
Horse-chestnut
Aesculus hippocastanum

Family: Horsechestnut (Sapindaceae)

Height: 40–60' (12–18 m)

Tree: medium-sized tree with single trunk that is often divided low, spreading round crown

Leaf: palmate compound, 5–10" (12.5–25 cm) in length, oppositely attached, composed of 5–9 (usually 7) leaflets, each leaflet 4–10" (10–25 cm) long, widest above the middle, radiating from a central point, with a sharp-toothed margin, hairy below when young, lacking hairs when mature

Bark: dark brown, many furrows and scales, inner bark orange brown

Flower: white flower with yellow or orange center, ½–1" (1–2.5 cm) wide, upright in spike clusters, 8–12" (20–30 cm) long

Fruit: thick-walled leathery green capsule, rounded, 2" (5 cm) diameter, covered with pointed spines, in hanging clusters, splits in 3 sections, contains 1–3 smooth, non-edible, shiny chestnut-brown seeds

Fall Color: yellow

Origin/Age: non-native, introduced to the U.S. from Europe; 75–100 years

Habitat: wide variety of soils, sun

Range: planted in parks and yards

Stan's Notes: Closely related to Ohio Buckeye (pg. 319). A remedy made from the seeds was used to treat cough in horses, hence its species and common names, *Hippo* ("Horse") and *Kastanon* ("chestnut"). The chemical esculin has been extracted from its leaves and bark for use in skin protectants. Also called Chestnut.

cross section

bark

flower

fruit

Yellow Buckeye
Aesculus flava

Family: Horsechestnut (Sapindaceae)

Height: 50–70' (15–21 m)

Tree: single or multiple trunks with spreading branches, round crown

Leaf: palmate compound, 5–14" (12.5–36 cm) in length, oppositely attached, composed of 5–7 leaflets, each leaflet 4–6" (10–15 cm) long, radiates from a central point, evenly fine-toothed, yellowish green above, lighter below, often hairy, short stalk (petiole)

Bark: brown to gray, thin

Flower: green-to-tan tubular flower, 1¼" (3 cm) long, in triangular clusters, 4–6" (10–15 cm) tall

Fruit: smooth, leathery, 3-parted, light brown capsule, round, 2–3" (5–7.5 cm) wide, thin husk, contains 1–2 poisonous seeds

Fall Color: yellow to orange

Origin/Age: native; 60–80 years

Habitat: deep moist soils, river and mountain valleys

Range: western quarter of the Carolinas, planted in parks

Stan's Notes: The largest and tallest buckeye. Never in pure stands in the Carolinas and confined to rich bottomlands. Commercial species sold as a shade tree. Looks like Ohio Buckeye (pg. 319) but is larger with smooth fruit capsules and hairier leaf undersides. Its soft wood is rated at the bottom of 35 leading timbers of the U.S. Pale yellow wood is used for pulpwood, artificial limbs and interior finishes for homes. Seeds and young shoots are poisonous and make livestock ill. Occurs in a wide variety of habitats up to 6,000 feet (1,830 m). Common tree of the Great Smoky Mountains. Also called Sweet Buckeye, Big Buckeye or Large Buckeye.

fruit

bark

flower

Ohio Buckeye
Aesculus glabra

Family: Horsechestnut (Sapindaceae)

Height: 20–40' (6–12 m)

Tree: single trunk, broad round crown with flat top

Leaf: palmate compound, 5–15" (12.5–37.5 cm) long, oppositely attached, composed of 5 leaflets, each leaflet 3–5" (7.5–12.5 cm) long, radiating from a central point, with fine irregular teeth, yellowish green above, pale and hairy below, sessile

Bark: brown with scaly patches, rough shallow furrows

Flower: green flower, ½" (1 cm) wide, growing upright in triangular clusters, 5–7" (12.5–18 cm) long, foul odor when crushed

Fruit: light brown spiny capsule, round, 1–2" (2.5–5 cm) wide, contains 1–2 shiny brown poisonous seeds

Fall Color: yellow to orange

Origin/Age: non-native; 100–125 years

Habitat: moist soils, river bottoms, sun to partial shade

Range: planted throughout in parks, yards and along streets

Stan's Notes: Also known as Fetid Buckeye or Stinking Buckeye, referring to the foul odor of the flowers and most other parts of the tree when crushed. Grows naturally in moist areas. Planted as a landscape tree in dry upland areas for its attractive autumn foliage. Its large poisonous seeds are avoided by wildlife. A unique palmate leaf, the leaflets lack their own leafstalks, all rising instead from a central stalk. An extract from the bark was once used as a stimulant for the cerebrospinal system. Once thought a buckeye seed carried in the pocket would ward off rheumatism. Warty spines on its fruit capsules help distinguish it from Yellow Buckeye (pg. 317).

skirt

boots

bark

flower

fruit

Cabbage Palmetto
Sabal palmetto

Family: Palm (Arecaceae)

Height: 30–50' (9–15 m)

Tree: medium-sized tree with single unbranched trunk, large round crown

Leaf: palmate compound, fan-shaped, 4–7' (1–2.1 m) long, up to 4' (1 m) wide, alternately attached, emerging directly from trunk, long stiff narrow segments, thread-like fibers separating from edges, evergreen, dull green, long leafstalk (petiole), up to 5' (1.5 m) long

Bark: gray to tan, many horizontal ridges

Flower: hundreds of small white to cream flowers, round, ⅓" (.8 cm) wide, in hanging clusters usually near the crown, 2' (.6 m) long, fragrant

Fruit: green berry (drupe), turning nearly black when mature, round, ⅓" (.8 cm) wide, containing 1 brown seed

Fall Color: green, leaves turn brown individually year-round

Origin/Age: native; 50–100 years

Habitat: dry sandy soils, open fields, full sun

Range: along the coast of the Carolinas, planted in parks

Stan's Notes: The state tree and displayed on state flag of South Carolina, the Palmetto State. Leaves grow directly from trunk, with old leaf bases, called boots (see inset), often remaining attached. Plants such as orchids, ferns and mosses grow in organic debris that collects in the boots. Dead leaves, if not trimmed, will hang from trunk and form a "skirt." It flowers in June and produces fruit by late fall to early winter. Fruit are a favorite food of many bird and mammal species. Also called Cabbage Palm or Sabal Palm.

GLOSSARY

Acorn: A nut, typically of oak trees, as in the White Oak. See *nut* and *fruit*.

Aggregate fruit: A fruit composed of multiple tiny berries, such as a mulberry, raspberry or blackberry. See *fruit*.

Alternate: A type of leaf attachment in which the leaves are singly and alternately attached along a stalk, as in Quaking Aspen.

Arcuate: Curved in form, like a bow, as in veins of Alternate-leaf Dogwood leaves.

Asymmetrical leaf base: A base of a leaf with lobes unequal in size or shape, as in elms. See *leaf base*.

Berry: A fleshy fruit with several seeds within, such as European Buckthorn. See *fruit*.

Bract: A petal-like structure on a flower, as in Blue Beech.

Branch: The smaller, thinner, woody parts of a tree, usually bearing the leaves and flowers.

Bristle-tipped: A type of leaf lobe ending in a projection, usually a sharply pointed tip, as in Red Oak.

Buttress: A wide or flared base of a tree trunk that helps to hold the tree upright in unstable soils, as in Bald Cypress.

Capsule: A dry fruit that opens along several seams to release the seeds within, as in Ohio Buckeye. See *pod*.

Catkin: A scaly cluster of usually same sex flowers, as in Bigtooth Aspen or any willow.

Chambered pith: The central soft part of a twig that is broken into spaced sections. See *pith*.

Clasping: A type of leaf attachment without a leafstalk in which the leaf base grasps the main stalk, partly surrounding the stalk at the point of attachment.

Clustered needles: A group of needles emanating from a central point, usually within a papery sheath, as in pine trees.

Compound leaf: A single leaf composed of at least 2 but usually not more than 20 leaflets growing along a single leafstalk, as in Smooth Sumac.

Cone: A cluster of woody scales encasing multiple nutlets or seeds and growing on a central stalk, as in coniferous trees.

Cone scale: An individual overlapping projection, often woody, on a cone, as in Austrian Pine.

Conifer: A type of tree that usually does not shed all of its leaves each autumn, such as pine or spruce.

Crooked: Off center or bent in form, not straight, as in a Black Locust trunk.

Deciduous: A type of tree that usually sheds all of its leaves each autumn, such as White Oak or Sugar Maple.

Dioecious: A type of tree that has male and female flowers on separate trees of the same species, as in Quaking Aspen. See *monoecious.*

Disk: A flattened, disk-like fruit that contains a seed, as in the American Elm. See *samara.*

Double-toothed margin: A jagged or serrated leaf edge that is composed of two types of teeth, usually one small and one large, as in Siberian Elm.

Drupe: A fleshy fruit that usually has a single seed, such as a cherry. See *fruit.*

Flower: To bloom, or produce a flower or flowers as a means of reproduction, as in deciduous trees.

Fruit: A ripened ovary or reproductive structure that contains one or more seeds, such as a nut or berry.

Furrowed: Having longitudinal channels or grooves, as in Swamp White Oak bark.

Gall: An abnormal growth of plant tissue that is usually caused by insects, microorganisms or injury.

Intolerant: Won't thrive in a particular condition, such as shade.

Lance-shaped: Long, narrow and pointed in form, like a spearhead, as in Weeping Willow leaves.

Leaf base: The area where a leafstalk attaches to the leaf.

Leaflet: One of the two or more leaf-like parts of a compound leaf, as in White Ash.

Leafstalk: The stalk of a leaf, extending from the leaf base to the branch. See *petiole*.

Lenticel: A small growth, usually on bark, that allows air into the interior of a tree, as in Paper Birch.

Lobed leaf: A single leaf with at least one indentation (sinus or notch) along an edge that does not reach the center or base of the leaf, as in oaks or maples.

Margin: The edge of a leaf.

Midrib: The central vein of a leaf, often more pronounced and larger in size than other veins, as in Black Cherry.

Monoecious: A type of tree that has male and female flowers on the same tree, as in Paper Birch. See *dioecious*.

Naturalized: Not originally native, growing and reproducing in the wild freely now, such as Russian-olive.

Needle: A long, usually thin, evergreen leaf of a conifer.

Notch: A small indentation along the margin of a leaf, as in Red Maple.

Nut: A large fruit encased by hard walls, usually containing one seed, such as an acorn. See *fruit*.

Nutlet: A small or diminutive nut or seed, usually contained in a cone or cone-like seed catkin, as in Red Pine or Paper Birch. See *fruit*.

Obovate: Shaped like an egg and flat, as in Pawpaw leaves.

Opposite: A type of leaf attachment in which leaves are situated directly across from each other on a stalk, as in Sugar Maple.

Ovate: Shaped like an egg, as in Austrian Pine cones.

Palmate compound leaf: A single leaf that is composed of three or more leaflets emanating from a common central point at the end of the leafstalk, as in Ohio Buckeye.

Petiole: The stalk of a leaf. See *leafstalk*.

Petiolule: The stalk of a leaflet in a compound leaf.

Pitch pocket: A raised blister that contains a thick resinous sap, as in Balsam Fir bark.

Pith: The central soft part of a twig in a young branch, turning to hard wood when mature.

Pod: A dry fruit that contains many seeds and opens at maturity, as in Kentucky Coffeetree. See *capsule*.

Pollination: The transfer of pollen from the male anther to the female stigma, usually resulting in the production of seeds.

Pome: A fleshy fruit with several chambers that contain many seeds, such as an apple. See *fruit*.

Rachis: The central or main stalk of a compound leaf, as in the European Mountain-ash.

Samara: A winged fruit that contains a seed, as in maples, ashes or elms. See *disk* and *fruit*.

Seed catkin: A small cone-like structure that contains nutlets or seeds, as in birches.

Sessile: Lacking a stalk and attaching directly at the base, as in Common Hoptree leaflets.

Simple leaf: A single leaf with an undivided or unlobed edge, as in American Elm.

Sinus: The recess or space in between two lobes of a leaf, as in the Red Oak.

Spine: A stiff, usually short, sharply pointed woody outgrowth from a branch or cone, as in Pitch Pine cones. See *thorn*.

Stalk: A thin structure that attaches a leaf, flower or fruit to a twig or branch.

Sucker: A secondary shoot produced from the base or roots of a tree that gives rise to a new plant, as in Quaking Aspen.

Tannin: A bitter-tasting chemical found within acorns and other parts of a tree, as in oaks.

Taproot: The primary, vertically descending root of a mature tree.

Terminal: Growing at the end of a stalk or branch.

Thorn: A stiff, usually long and sharply pointed woody outgrowth from a branch or trunk, as in American Plum. See *spine*.

Tolerant: Will thrive in a particular condition, such as shade.

Understory: The small trees and other plants that grow under a canopy of larger trees; the shady habitat beneath a forest canopy.

Whorl: A ring of three or more leaves, stalks or branches arising from a common point, as in Red Pine or Southern Catalpa.

Winged: Having thin appendages, attached to a seed, branch or twig, as in maple seeds or Winged Elm.

Woody: Composed of wood, as in trees or cones. See *cone scale.*

Photo credits *(continued from page ii)*

The following Bugwood (weedimages.org) images below are licensed under the Creative Commons Attribution 3.0 (CC BY 3.0 US) License.
Franklin Bonner/USFS: 118 (fruit), 128 (fruit), 138 (fruit), 232 (fruit), 252 (fruit); **Charles T. Bryson/USDA Agricultural Research Service:** 70 (flower); **Bill Cook/MI State University:** 184 (fruit), 206 (flower); **Keith Kanoti/Maine Forest Service:** 202 (flower); **James H. Miller & Ted Bodner; Southern Weed Science Society:** 312 (fruit); **Pennsylvania Department of Conservation and Natural Resources, Forestry:** 220 (fruit); and **Rob Routledge/Sault College:** 214 (flower).

The following Bugwood (weedimages.org) images below are licensed under the Creative Commons Attribution Non-Commerical 3.0 (CC BY-NC 3.0 US) License.
William M. Ciesla/Forest Health Management International: 320 (flower); **Troy Evans/Great Smoky Mountains National Park:** 306 (fruit); **Dow Gardens:** 214 (fruit); **Brian Lockhart/USDA Forest Service:** 142 (fruit); **Karan A. Rawlins, University of Georgia:** 280 (bark); and **John Ruter, University of Georgia:** 30 (main), 140 (bark), 142 (immature fruit), 186 (flower), 258 (flower).

Images used under license from Shutterstock.com:
Eleonimages: 218 (flower); **Islavicek:** 224 (fruit); **Nikolay Kurzenko:** 198 (flower), 222 (fruit); **Lightrain:** 184 (flower); **Bruce MacQueen:** 136 (flower); **Wiert nieuman:** 268 (fruit); **J Need:** 146 (flower); **simona pavan:** 272 (flower); **Puffin's Pictures:** 90 (flower); **Jordi Roy:** 86 (fruit), 218 (fruit); **Sambhatharu:** 150 (fruit); **Shigeyoshi Umezu:** 108 (fruit); **Iva Vagnerova:** 268 (flower); and **Iva Villi:** 316 (flower).

CHECKLIST/INDEX

Use the boxes to check trees you've seen.

MORE FOR THE SOUTH BY STAN TEKIELA

Identification Guides
Birds of the Carolinas Field Guide

Birds of Prey of the South
Field Guide

Wildflowers of the Carolinas
Field Guide

Wildflowers of the Southeast
Field Guide

Children's Books:
Adventure Board Book Series
Floppers & Loppers

Paws & Claws

Peepers & Peekers

Snouts & Sniffers

Children's Books
C is for Cardinal

Can You Count the Critters?

Critter Litter

Children's Books:
Wildlife Picture Books
Baby Bear Discovers the World

The Cutest Critter

Do Beavers Need Blankets?

Hidden Critters

Jump, Little Wood Ducks

Some Babies Are Wild

Super Animal Powers

What Eats That?

Whose Baby Butt?

Whose Butt?

Whose Track Is That?

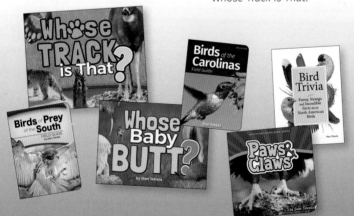